Praise for *Simply Brilliant*

'I have been working with Fergus and using Simply Brilliant *for 10 years now – it does not fail. Many books will tell you why,* Simply Brilliant *tells you how; how to cut to the heart of getting things done, the key to succeeding in manufacturing and service industries.'*
Tim Starr, Site Director, Abbott Vascular, Switzerland

'*After attending one of Fergus's seminars, I was immediately struck by the value of the training content and the ease with which insights could be implemented for personal, team and program benefit.* Simply Brilliant *is a compelling read and educational tool. The information is presented in a practical, easy-to-follow manner with clear recommendations on things to do to be successful. Further, the narrative uniquely captures Fergus's personality and essence of his training experience. I would highly recommend* Simply Brilliant *to people and organisations who are truly motivated to upgrade their ability to deliver on increasingly complex assignments.'*
Conor Twomey Ph.D., R&D Director, Scott Safety, North Carolina

'*It is always good to find a book that does what it says in the title, and* Simply Brilliant *is one of these. Since the first edition, this book has been a permanent reference and is now a recommended read for all staff members.'*
Noel Kelly FRSA, Chief Executive Officer/Director, Visual Artists Ireland

Simply
Brilliant

Simply Brilliant

The common-sense guide to success at work

Fourth edition

FERGUS O'CONNELL

PEARSON

Harlow, England • London • New York • Boston • San Francisco • Toronto • Sydney
Auckland • Singapore • Hong Kong • Tokyo • Seoul • Taipei • New Delhi
Cape Town • São Paulo • Mexico City • Madrid • Amsterdam • Munich • Paris • Milan

650.1

OCO

PEARSON EDUCATION LIMITED

Edinburgh Gate
Harlow CM20 2JE
Tel: +44 (0)1279 623623
Fax: +44 (0)1279 431059
Website: www.pearson.com/uk

First published in Great Britain in 2001
Second edition published 2004
Third edition published 2008
Fourth edition published 2012

Pearson Education is not responsible for the content of third-party internet sites.

ISBN: 978-0-273-76808-1

British Library Cataloguing-in-Publication Data
A catalogue record for this book is available from the British Library

Library of Congress Cataloging-in-Publication Data
O'Connell, Fergus.
 Simply brilliant : the common-sense guide to success at work / Fergus O'connell.
 -- 4th ed.
   p. cm.
 Rev. ed. of: Simply brilliant : the competitive advantage of common sense. 3rd ed.
 Includes bibliographical references.
 ISBN 978-0-273-76808-1 (pbk.)
 1. Executive ability--Problems, exercises, etc. 2. Common sense--Problems,
 exercises, etc. 3. Simplicity--Problems, exercises, etc. 4. Management--Problems,
 exercises, etc. I. Title.
 HD38.2.03 2012
 658.4'09--dc23

                    2011047408

10 9 8 7 6 5 4 3 2 1
15 14 13 12

Design by Design Deluxe
Typeset in 9.5pt on 13pt Iowan Old Style BT Roman by 30
Printed and bound in Great Britain by Henry Ling Ltd, at the Dorset Press, Dorchester,
Dorset

For my beautiful wife Francine Carla Shannon

Contents

About the author

The *Sunday Business Post* has described **Fergus O'Connell** as having 'more strings to his bow than a Stradivarius'. He graduated from University College Cork with a First in Mathematical Physics.

Fergus is one of the world's leading authorities on project management and getting things done in the shortest possible time. His project management method – Structured Project Management/The Ten Steps – has influenced a generation of project managers. In 2003 the method was used to plan and execute the Special Olympics World Games, the world's biggest sporting event that year. His radical methods for shortening projects are in use by a growing band of devotees. His experience covers projects around the world; he has taught project management in Europe, North America, South America and Asia. He has written for the *Sunday Business Post*, *Computer Weekly* and the *Wall Street Journal*. He has lectured at University College Cork, Trinity College Dublin, Bentley College, Boston University, the Michael Smurfit Graduate School of Business and on television for the National Technological University.

Fergus is also a serial entrepreneur. In 1992, he founded ETP (**www.etpint.com**), now one of the world's leading programme and project management companies.

His latest venture is a publishing company Paper & Celluloid (**www.paperandcelluloid.com**), which will publish its first books later this year. Fergus holds two patents.

Fergus is the author of 12 business books. The first of these, *How to Run Successful Projects: The Silver Bullet*, has become both a bestseller and a classic and has been constantly in print for over 20 years. *Simply Brilliant* – also a bestseller – was runner-up in the WH Smith Book Awards 2002. His books have been translated into 20 languages.

Fergus has also written a book on project management for children. Entitled *How To Put A Man On The Moon If You're A Kid*, the book is one of a pair of books to teach the essential skills of project management and time management to schoolchildren. (The other, *How To Build Rome In A Day If You're A Kid*, is in the pipeline.)

Fergus' first love is writing fiction. His 2002 novel, *Call The Swallow*, was described by the *Irish Times* as 'better than *Schindler's Ark*' (itself a Booker Prize winner). *Call The Swallow* was short-listed for the 2002 Kerry Ingredients Irish Fiction Prize and nominated for the Hughes & Hughes/Sunday Independent Novel of the Year. His new novel, *Starlight*, has just been published.

He is married, has two children, three stepchildren and is moving to Ireland from France where he has lived for the last seven years.

Acknowledgements

This book is a project that I have been nursing for a long number of years. I think there was a part of me that always thought it was too wacky for any publisher to be interested in. I would talk to people about it and – it may have been my imagination – they would smile uncomfortably, and begin to move warily away. That it has finally seen the light of day is the result of one woman's belief in and passion for the project. That woman is my editor at Pearson Education, Rachael Stock. When Rachael called me to say 'everyone loved it' – 'it' being the book proposal – I think what she was really saying was that everyone had been infected by her enthusiasm for it. Rachael has been the perfect editor and I thank her for giving me the chance to write my book.

I'd like to offer the same thanks to Eloise Cook who has championed this edition.

Preface

Much of my adult life has been spent rubbing shoulders with smart people. In college, in every job I've ever been in, in starting businesses, these smart people have been colleagues, bosses, peers, customers. I believe this experience is true not only of myself. More and more of us are finding our lives affected by these selfsame smart people and the things they make and do.

Over the years a suspicion has gradually been growing on me. It is a suspicion that I have been slow to voice. However, as the years have gone by, and as the evidence has accumulated, I have finally come to the conclusion that despite smartness, expertise, skill, experience, genius, in some cases some (many?) of these people are lacking in an essential skill.

That skill is what I refer to in this book as 'common sense'.

'The trouble with common sense,' the old saw goes, 'is that it's not all that common.' That has very much been my experience. Despite all the smarts that are floating around the place, a lot of dumb things get done. These are things which, if we only applied some of this pixie dust we call common sense, would never have been allowed to happen.

Smart people seem to like complicated – complicated ideas, complicated processes and methods, complicated solutions to problems. Nothing wrong with that necessarily, except that complicated often equals:

- expensive to implement and maintain;
- not necessarily taking into account the fact that there are people involved;
- not necessarily good or the best; and
- sometimes just plain ... well, wrong.

It is against this background that I have written this little book. It sets down a number of rules of common sense. Rather than trying to *define* common sense, it tries to identify a bunch of things which, if one were doing them, one would be 'using common sense'.

I have taught these rules to many, many people over the years and seen them achieve real benefits with them. The rules are applicable in any situation, whether in work or outside it, but the book focuses primarily on the workplace.

The 'promise' of the book is pretty simple. To a greater or a lesser extent, it will give you a new way of looking at the world. It will give you new ways of finding solutions to problems – ways which are both simple and fast. And if it stops *you* from doing some dumb things then that will have been a blessing indeed.

Introduction

The book identifies seven 'rules' of common sense – rules which will enable you to stop overcomplicating the issues that you encounter every day.

In keeping with the first of the seven rules – that many things are simple – the book is simple. There are seven chapters. Each chapter follows the same organisation:

- **Questions** At the beginning of each chapter there are some questions to get you thinking. In a sense, these questions test whether and how much you think in a common-sense sort of way.

- **The rule** Here I outline the concept of the chapter.

- **How to** Shows you how to apply the rule.

- **Examples/Applications** These are examples of applying the particular rule. These could relate to one particular rule, or several in combination.

- **What should you do?** Finally, there are some action points or things you could do to begin applying that particular rule in your daily life.

I'd like to know if you found the book useful or if it made any kind of difference. Or not! With that in mind you can email me at **fergus.oconnell@etpint.com** with any brickbats or bouquets (or anything in between).

Finally, a note on terminology. I use the words 'project', 'venture' and 'undertaking' interchangeably in this book. They all are taken to mean something that you're trying to do.

Chapter

Many things are simple

This chapter extols the virtues of simplicity in our thinking and encourages us to seek simple solutions.

Questions

Before you read on, spend a few moments thinking about and answering the following:

1. Somebody who works for you has a major body odour problem. Several of your other employees have complained about it. What should you do?

2. You have the feeling that your customer service is not what it was or not as good as your competitors'. What should you do?

The rule

I'll freely accept that some things in life are not simple. Putting a man on the moon, for example, or the Apollo 13 rescue were immensely complex feats of engineering, mathematics, computing, rocketry, physics and many other disciplines.

However, you may have heard the expression, 'It's not rocket science.' Launching, flying and returning the Space Shuttle to Earth *is* rocket science and requires the application of a lot of complex scientific and technological thought. But most of us aren't flight directors at NASA and the things we do are definitely not rocket science. Too often, I believe we look for complex solutions when simple ones would be (a) much more appropriate, (b) much easier to find and (c) much simpler to implement.

"Too often, I believe we look for complex solutions"

Consider the two questions at the head of the chapter. For question 1, I've had answers like, 'Send out a general email about dress code and see if they'll take the hint', 'Hand it over to Human Resources', 'Launch a dress code/grooming initiative.' With all due respect, such answers are a bit daft in comparison to the rather obvious, 'Take them aside, tell them what the problem is and ask them to do something about it.'

Similarly, for question 2, the best (and cheapest) answer I've ever heard to it is, 'Ask your people to treat each customer as though they were a friend, i.e. somebody they would not want to let down.'

It has to be said that an awful lot of people seem to love complex. I mean, does anyone understand – in the sense that they can compare – mobile phone pricing rates? Or the different types of rail tickets and associated prices? And what about the design of most of the computer systems we have to use? Or think of the great sense of gloom that descends upon us when we have to deal with a government agency – we know we may as well set aside hours for our search through the labyrinth until we find the person or department that can deal with our issue. And let's not forget the Lisbon Treaty – the document that amends a number of existing European Union (EU) treaties to give the EU its constitution. The result is more than 3,000 pages. I mean, how difficult can it be to say, 'We're a bunch of countries and we'd like to cooperate on a bunch of things'?

And then sometimes – wonderfully – we discover something simple. I came across a package recently for doing mind mapping. I had tried such packages before but always gave up on them. This one I was able to use within a minute. It was completely intuitive. I was so stunned I called up the makers to thank them. Or go book an airline ticket on a Ryanair flight and see how uncomplicated it is in comparison to almost any other airline.

How to

If you are ever lucky enough to hear the Israeli scientist Eli Goldratt speak, he will almost certainly tell you what he calls 'one of the fundamental beliefs of science'. As he puts it, 'In reality there are no complex systems' or 'Reality cannot be complex.' Therefore our first rule of common sense says that you need to shun complexity and seek simplicity. The following can all help you to do this:

- Look for simple solutions.

- Ask: 'What would be the simplest thing to do here?'

- See if you can describe something – an issue, a problem, a solution, a proposal – coherently in 25 words or less.

- Or can you do it in 30 seconds? This is sometimes called the 'elevator story' or 'elevator pitch', the idea being that you meet some important person in an elevator and you've got the flight time of the elevator to convey your message.

- Write down the issue/problem/solution/proposal.

- If you find you have ended up with a complex solution or idea, you have probably gone in the wrong direction. Go back and look again, this time in the simple direction.

- When you come up with something, ask: 'Is there a simpler way?'

- Get people to 'tell it like I'm a six-year-old'.

- Ask simple questions. Who? What? Why? Where? When? How? Which?

- Ask for simple answers. This is particularly important when you are dealing with highly technical people.

- Remember the acronym 'KISS' – Keep It Simple, Stupid.

- Learn and use lateral thinking. The need for lateral thinking arises out of the way the mind works. The mind acts to create, recognise and use patterns. It does not act to *change* patterns. Lateral thinking is all about changing patterns. It is about escaping from old ideas and generating new ones. Lateral thinking involves two basic processes:

  - escape;

  - provocation.

- Escape is about recognising the current received wisdom with regard to something and then searching for alternative ways to look at or do that thing. Provocation is about finding those alternative ways.

- Learn to think like Leonardo Da Vinci. In the book *How to Think Like Leonardo Da Vinci*, the author, Michael Gelb, identifies what he calls 'the fundamentals of Leonardo's approach to learning and the cultivation of intelligence'. Go read it.

"Lateral thinking is all about changing patterns"

Examples/Applications

Example 1 Running a successful business

How do you run a successful business? They say it's complicated. There are business schools out there to enable you to do it properly. All manner of complex research has been done in the area. Could you describe it in five minutes, in a page, in a sentence?

You actually could, and Eileen Shapiro does precisely that in her book *The Seven Deadly Sins of Business*. She describes the professor entering her first finance class in business school and saying to the wannabe investment bankers and corporate executives: 'Don't run out of cash.' Is this the recipe for a successful business? You bet it is.

Example 2 Marketing

Before I started my own company, I used to think that marketing was about sharp suits, power lunches, advertising hype and having to be nice to potential customers. I now realise it's one of the most complex, precise and demanding disciplines on earth. And yet, simplicity is the key to it. The key to being good at marketing is to be able to explain – *very simply* – why someone should buy what you sell. So how would you do this? Well, imagine you had to explain your idea to a six-year-old. How would you do it? What would be your angle/how would you pitch it so as to grab their attention? What words would you use? What words could you *not* use because they are too complicated or jargon?

If you can 'tell it to me like I'm a six-year-old' then you will be a great marketer.

"Simplicity is the key to it"

Example 3 Lateral thinking

There's a story I heard which may well be apocryphal, but even if it is, it serves our purposes well at this point. It goes as follows.

A major US corporation built a new, high-rise corporate headquarters. A few weeks after the building was fully occupied, the employees began to complain about the slowness of the elevators. Very quickly, the complaints reached epidemic proportions, so the company spoke to the architects of the building. Could the lifts be speeded up? Or increased in size? Sure, came the reply, but it would involve months of demolition, extension and recon-struction around the elevator shafts. It would be hugely disruptive to a large part of the workforce.

Supposedly, the story goes, the corporation did nothing to the elevator shafts. Instead, it placed full-length mirrors on every floor beside the elevator doors. The employees spent an extra few moments preening themselves and looking at one another in the mirrors, and the complaints faded away.

The point of the story? There must be a simple solution. Look for it.

Example 4 Beware of meetings

In my experience, meetings can be particularly bad places for the complex versus simple discussion – places where the exponents of simple can fare badly. I once attended a meeting where a terrible decision was made.

In the early eighties I was part of a team that was developing a laptop computer. Today such devices are pieces of consumer electronics; in those days a machine like that would have been ground-breaking. It was the first of a few times in my life when I might have become rich.

There came the day when the decision as to what operating system the machine would run had to be made. There were two contenders. There was a technically very sophisticated solution and something called MS-DOS. Yes – you've guessed it – the techies triumphed and plumped for the sophisticated solution.

It would be several months before we realised what a catastrophic error we had made and that we weren't all going to be driving Ferraris after all!

So beware particularly of so-called 'group think' at meetings. If you find your meeting heading off down a road of complexity, try to stop the headlong charge. Ask the question, 'What would be the simplest thing to do here?' and see if you can't take things in a simpler (and potentially more useful) direction.

"Ask the question, 'What would be the simplest thing to do here?'"

AND SO, WHAT SHOULD YOU DO?

1. Look for simple solutions. Ask: 'What would be the simplest thing to do here?'

2. See if you can describe something – an issue, a problem, a solution, a proposal – coherently in 25 words or less. Or in 30 seconds. (This is essentially the concept of the 'elevator pitch', the idea being that you meet some important person in an elevator and you've got the flight time of the elevator to convey your message.) Or as though you were telling it to a six-year-old.

3. If you find you have ended up with a complex solution or idea, you have probably gone in the wrong direction. Go back and look again, this time in the simple direction.

4. Ask simple questions. Who? What? Why? Where? When? How? Which?

5. Ask for simple answers. This is particularly important when you are dealing with highly technical people.

6. Remember the acronym 'KISS' – Keep It Simple, Stupid.

7. Read:

   - Edward De Bono's book *Simplicity*; or

   - any of Edward De Bono's books on lateral thinking; or

   - *How to Think Like Leonardo Da Vinci* by Michael Gelb.

Chapter

2

Know what you're trying to do

This chapter makes the age-old point that if you don't know what port you're sailing to, then any wind is a fair wind.

Questions

Before you start this chapter try these on for size. Have a think and write down answers to them.

1. An urgent issue has cropped up with one of your customers. Its solution seems pretty straightforward. There is a meeting where your boss and the customer both utter the line, 'We don't have time to plan it – just go do it!' What's your first move?

2. You've nearly completed an order for a customer when he phones you to ask for 'one little extra' but still with delivery as originally agreed. The 'one little extra' is actually reasonably significant. You are new to the company. The customer tells you that your predecessor always accommodated such requests. What do you do?

The rule

'If you don't know what port you're sailing to,' the quote goes, conjuring up visions of sunny sea journeys in an unpolluted and empty Mediterranean, 'then any wind is a fair wind.'

The sentiment is so well known as to be clichéd. The quote is attributed to lots of different people. To the best of my knowledge it is not clear to whom attribution should go, other than the fact that it was first uttered a long time ago.

To put it more mundanely, if you don't know what you're trying to do, it's going to be hard to do it.

Or let's have it from Lewis Carroll in *Alice's Adventures in Wonderland*. Alice asks the Cheshire Cat:

> 'Would you tell me, please, which way I ought to go from here?'
>
> 'That depends a good deal on where you want to get to,' said the Cat.
>
> 'I don't much care where,' said Alice.
>
> 'Then, it doesn't matter which way you go,' said the Cat.

Whether it's a meeting, a presentation, a day, a week, a year, a life, a house renovation, an ambition, or whatever, if you don't know what you're trying to achieve with that meeting, presentation, day, week, year, life, house renovation, ambition, or whatever, it's going to be hard to do it.

If you start a meeting and don't know what you're trying to get out of it, the chances of you actually getting something useful, never mind something you actually wanted, from it are pretty remote. As for question 1 at the head of the chapter, if I could ask you to take only one thing away from this book, it is the idea that 'we don't have time to plan it – just go do it' is always wrong. A little planning is *always* better than a lot of firefighting. Figure out precisely what you've been asked to do (the subject of this chapter), build a plan (the subject of Chapters 3, 4 and 5) and then work the plan (Chapter 6). This will always ultimately take you less time than if you just go at something like a bull at a gate.

"A little planning is *always* better than a lot of firefighting"

We discuss the answer to question 2 in Example 4 'Healthy and unhealthy projects' later in this chapter. But can I just suggest at this stage that if you answered:

- say 'yes' – satisfying the customer is what it's all about, or

- ask the team to work some nights and weekends and have a moan with them about 'bloody customers',

then you were 100 per cent wrong.

How to

In knowing what you are trying to do, there are really two issues you have to concern yourself with. These are:

- understanding what you're trying to do;

- knowing if what you're trying to do is what everyone wants.

We'll also discuss the notion of visualisation.

Understand what you're trying to do

Somebody – your boss, say, or a customer – asks you to do something and you hare off straight away to do it. Right? Uh-uh. Bad move.

What you really want to do, before you do anything else, is to understand *precisely* what they've asked you to do. So ask yourself, 'What's the end of this project?' What is the event which, when it occurs, shows this project is over?

The ribbon cutting for a new store or bridge, the break-ing of a bottle of champagne on the side of a ship when it is being launched are examples of the event that marks the end of the project. By focusing on this point you can quickly see what's included in the project (sometimes called 'in scope') and what's not ('out of scope').

Know if what you're trying to do is what everyone wants

All projects, whether large or small, have what are known as 'stakeholders'. Stakeholders are the people who have a stake in the project. More specifically, they are the individ-uals or groups of people who are affected by the project in some way. Individuals can be stakeholders, e.g. Charlie is a stakeholder, or a group of people can be a stakeholder, e.g. all of our company's customers are a stakeholder.

Each stakeholder then has win-conditions. Win-conditions are those things that they want to get from the particu-lar venture or undertaking. For example, if I am the boss who has given the troops the impossible deadline, then my win-condition is that they hit the deadline. If, on the other hand, I am a team member who has been working burn-out hours for the last six months, then maybe my win-condition is that I just want to work a 40-hour week.

"It's all about 'happy stakeholders'"

A successful project can be summed up in two words – it's all about 'happy stakeholders'. You tell the stakeholders what they're going to get and that's what they get. Clearly then, the first step in delivering happy stakeholders is to understand what they want. So go ask them. And don't assume that you know. Or that they all want the same thing. Or that all of the stakeholders are of equal importance. Make a list of all of your stakeholders and write down their win-conditions. Does the project that you've envisioned in the previous section deliver all of these win-conditions? If not then you'll either have to add them in or tell the stakeholders that certain win-conditions can't/won't be met.

We will see this notion again in Chapter 7.

Visualisation

Visualisation is all about trying to imagine what things will be like. Maybe, in some ways, daydreaming is a better word. Visualisation is a powerful technique because it forces you to see what you're trying to do from many different perspectives. It can have dramatic and wide-ranging effects. In particular, visualising what you're trying to do can have the following effects:

- It helps you to identify the goal of a project or venture in the first place.

- It tightens the definition of that goal, identifying things which lie within the scope of the venture and things which lie outside it.

- As we will see in the first example overleaf, it starts the planning process – the transition from the what (we are trying to do) to the how (we will do it).

- It can be a huge motivator to all those involved in the project, as we paint the picture of where we are heading, what we will have achieved when we get there and what the journey there will be like.

If you want a great example of visualisation, check out Martin Luther King's 'I Have A Dream' speech in Washington in 1963.

Examples/Applications

Example 1 Figuring out what you've been asked to do

Let's try to illustrate all of the above with an example. Let's assume your organisation is expanding, you need more people and you've decided to run a job advertisement. Seems straightforward enough. Write the ad, run it and deal with the fallout from it. Let's see if applying our tools adds any value or provides us with any new insights.

Let's first attempt to understand what we're trying to do. What event marks the end of this project? This is actually a very interesting question, and the answer is not at all as obvious as it might first appear. Are we finished when the ad runs? Or when we've processed the results? Or run the interviews? Or hired the people? Or something else? If we spend large amounts of the company's money to run an ad, and we end up getting no responses, has this been a success? Do we care? (On the basis that it's not our money!) If our existing people see an ad, will there be issues about salary scales or job descriptions or conditions? If the hiring of the people lies within the scope of what we are doing, then will we have to involve other people – the Human Resources department, for example? I hope you can see that by asking the 'What event marks the end of this project?' question, we find that this business of 'running an ad' is not at all as one-dimensional and well defined as it may have appeared at first glance.

Now let's assume we decide that 'running the ad' will mean precisely that. It will encompass just the business of getting the ad into a particular newspaper. Anything else – processing the results, arranging and carrying out interviews, making job offers – will form part of a new little project or projects. (Notice that this is completely arbitrary on our part – we could have chosen differently and still have been right.) So, we now know the answer to the question, 'What event marks the end point?' It's when the ad appears in the *Hamster and Furry Rodent Weekly* or wherever it is you're planning to run it.

And who are the stakeholders and what are their win-conditions? Well, there's:

- us – we want to run an ad that reflects well on the company. It should communicate why the jobs on offer are so attractive that you'd have to be mad not to apply. We also want all of the other stakeholders to be happy;

- our boss – they want the ad to send out a positive message about the company. Imagine her opening the paper and reading an ad that she, for whatever reason, turned out to be unhappy with. (So reviews and proof-reading will be required. Notice how this thought process begins to bridge us from the *what* we are trying to do to the *how* we will do it.) Our boss can perhaps act as a proxy for all other higher-ups – bigger bosses, shareholders, etc.;

- our existing employees – we need to make sure that anything that appears in the ad is in the public domain within the company. In other words, that nobody who already works in our company should be taken by surprise by the ad or find out things for the first time in it;

- potential employees – the ad needs to send out a message that the company is one that people want to work for;

- our customers – hey, maybe we didn't expect these guys to be here, but it's true. Existing and potential customers will read the ad, so it must say to them that the company is expanding and is a good company to do business with;

- the newspaper – it needs to receive the ad in a form it can accept.

Example 2 Meetings

Here's another example of knowing what you're trying to do.

Survey after survey affirms that most managers consider meetings to be the single biggest waste of their time. So write the minutes of meetings *before* the meeting. In doing this you will focus very clearly on the result you are trying to get from the meeting. You will be saying, 'Here's how I will know when this meeting has achieved its objectives.'

This idea of 'What result are we trying to achieve?' is one that can be extended to all sorts of things:

- presentations;
- customer visits or sales calls;
- project status reports – write it *before* the period to which it is going to refer. Will having it in front of you keep you focused? You bet it will;
- the day ahead of you.

Example 3 Setting goals

The visualisation tool is probably the best way I know to go about setting goals, be they business or personal ones. And this notion is not a new idea. Nearly 500 years ago, Pope Leo X complained about Leonardo Da Vinci: 'Here is a man, alas, who will never do anything, since he is thinking of the completion of his painting before he has started.' This idea of thinking about the end is also enshrined in one of Stephen Covey's '7 habits'. Habit 2 is 'Begin with the end in mind'. Visualisation is a great way of doing precisely that.

"We are all familiar with visualisation"

In a sense we are all familiar with visualisation. If we've ever daydreamed, then we've been engaging in visualisation. In daydreams we run little movie clips in our heads and in them we see ourselves doing things we really want to do. To begin setting personal goals, the best way to start is to picture what life will be like when that particular goal is achieved. Here are the kind of questions you could ask yourself to get the daydream (or movie clip) rolling:

- There will come a day when this goal has been achieved. What will life be like on that day? How will you spend it? Think through such a day from getting up in the morning to when you go to bed at night. How will you feel?

- What will your ambitions/hopes/dreams be on that day?

- Will your standard of living have changed? If it is a business goal, will your position within the organisation have changed?

- Will you have power, capabilities, other assets or a view of yourself that you don't have at the moment?

- Are there other people who will be affected by this goal? Who are they? (From a business point of view, think bosses, peers, customers, subordinates, team members, other parts of the organisation. From a personal point of view, there are nearest and dearest, family, friends, acquaintances.) How will these other people be affected by the goal? What will reaching this goal mean to each of them?

- Why do you want to achieve this goal?

- What will other people be saying about you – both the people who are affected by the goal and those who aren't affected but who know you?

- What recognition, if any, are you hoping to achieve in going for this goal?

- Do you think it is a difficult task you have set yourself? Could it fail? How would you feel then?

Example 4 Healthy and unhealthy projects

So far we've talked about the goals of projects as though they were static but, of course, the world isn't like that. Sometimes, almost as soon as we have firmed up on what the stakeholders want and begun the project, things start to change. Other issues emerge that they should have told us about but they didn't; there are things we should have seen but we missed; the business climate changes or our competitors do something we have to respond to; or the powers-that-be take people from our project to put them on another project, etc. Change – that's life on the project.

When these changes occur it's important for you to realise that there are three – and only three – ways that you can respond to these changes. They are:

1. You can say, 'Hey, that's a big change. That's not what was originally agreed.' Increases in the scope of the project, reductions in the staffing and assumptions turning out not to be true ('We assumed we'd only be doing this in three locations, we're now doing it in seven') are all examples of big changes.

2. You can use contingency (spare time or spare budget or spare manpower – see Chapter 5 for more on this) that you were smart enough to build into your plan and not dumb enough to let people remove.

3. You can suck it up – work nights, work weekends, get the team to work nights and weekends, bring work home with you, etc.

On a *healthy* project all three of these things get done. (Yes, I have no ideological problem with point 3 – to hit a deadline, to solve a customer problem. But I do have a problem when it is the only way that changes are dealt with.) On an *unhealthy* project, all changes are dealt with by sucking it up. We've all worked on such projects at times in our lives. They're not fun.

Example 5 'This shouldn't take you very long ...'

Have you ever had this happen to you? Somebody gives you something to do and says that it's small, it shouldn't take you very long, it's just a little thing. Two years later you find yourself still working on it because it turned out to be bigger than the Aswan Dam.

To avoid this, when somebody hands you one of these supposedly little things in the future – just make a list of all of its stakeholders. If you find yourself getting up to around six or more stakeholders then this is nature's way of saying that maybe this little baby isn't at all as small as everybody may have thought.

Example 6 Making sure your objectives are achievable

Here's an objective that I came across recently. A very senior executive in a very large company is going to be measured on this at the end of the year:

'To increase the accountability of Operations and reduce the need for QA second review and approval.'

What's the problem? Well, the problem is – who knows exactly what this means? And what's likely to happen? What's likely to happen is that the executive in question will work away on activities/tasks/projects which she believes are furthering this objective. When the end of the year comes, her boss will assess her progress against this objective. But what are the chances that his view of what she has achieved and hers line up 100 per cent? Very low, I would have said, because the way the objective is phrased is open to all sorts of interpretation.

So if you have this problem – if you have vague objectives like, 'Get the projects done' or 'Keep the customers happy' or 'Make the world a better place for little furry animals', you'd better get on it. Because you're going to be faced with the same problem. You'll bust your ass working towards the particular objectives only to find that you weren't quite working on the right things.

So – go have the discussion with your boss that begins with the words, 'Hey boss, when the end of the year comes, how would we *both* know that I've done an *amazing* job?' Then use the tools we have described in this chapter to tease out what the measures of this amazing performance would be. With something like, say, a sales target, it's easy. But the success measures of all jobs can be teased out. It just takes a bit of effort. And *you'll* have to initiate it – because, in all likelihood, your boss won't. But I hope you can see the benefits of doing so – because if you do then every scrap of work you do will build towards the achievement of your objectives and there will be no wasted effort on your part.

"It just takes a bit of effort"

AND SO, WHAT SHOULD YOU DO?

1. Keep a list of the things you're trying to do – your 'projects'.

2. Use the tools we have described in the 'How to' section of this chapter to analyse new things as they come along, and before adding them to your list of projects.

3. Run only healthy projects. Make the right choice (from the three choices) when changes occur on your projects.

Chapter

3

There is always a sequence of events

This chapter shows that in order to do anything, there needs to be a sequence of events. Knowing this gives you the skills to plan, prioritise, accelerate projects and get many things done at the same time. It also shows how 'firefighting' can become the exception rather than the rule.

Questions

Do you agree with the following statements?

1. When planning a project, the conventional wisdom is that you can only plan in detail for the next phase of the project and after that, it's pretty much guesswork.

2. You're dealing with a lawyer and when you ask him how long a piece of the legal process is going to take, he answers, 'How long is a piece of string?' or 'It'll take as long as it takes.' This is an acceptable answer since some things are just like that.

The rule

But first, just to get the questions out of the way – if you agreed with either of these statements then you were completely, 100 per cent wrong. Read on to find out more.

A few years ago, two people I knew decided to take their children to Disneyland Paris. They explained their plan to me. It went like this. They would fly to Paris on Friday evening, arriving late. On Saturday morning, after breakfast, they would travel out from central Paris to Disneyland, spend the day there, visit all the good rides, come back, put the children to bed with a babysitter, have a bath to wind down, dress up, go out and have a nice relaxing dinner.

My immediate reaction was, 'That's gonna be one long day.' I guess it's the project manager in me, but it sounded like that Saturday wouldn't come to a close until well into Sunday. When I mentally strung all the tasks together, there seemed to be an awful lot going on there. When I did it on paper, my suspicions were confirmed. Here's what their Saturday was going to look like. *Best* case.

Depart hotel	9:00	With kids in tow, you'll be doing well if you achieve this.
Paris – Disneyland	9:00 – 11:00	
A day at Disneyland	11:00 – 19:00	Has to be a minimum of eight hours.
Disneyland – Paris	19:00 – 21:00	
Kids to bed	21:00 – 23:00	You can't just rush them off to bed when you get back.
Bath to wind down	23:00 – 24:00	Has to be at least an hour to get the value of it at all.
Dress up	24:00 – 01:00	It's now Sunday.
Find / get to restaurant	01:00 – 01:30	Assuming there's one that's open in the middle of the night! Hey, it's Paris – there has to be!
Nice relaxing dinner	01:30 – 04:30	Say three hours. At this stage the diners will have been up for close on 24 hours! Relaxed? I'd say they'll be comatose!

The point of this story is not to show that anyone was stupid. The point is that there is always a sequence of events, and many people either don't realise this or, if they do, don't seem to understand the implications of the sequence of events.

For some reason – I think it's something I got from my father – I'm very precise and, I guess, old-fashioned about time. If I tell somebody I'll meet them at 3 o'clock, I'll be there before 3.00. If they're not there at 3.00, I'll quickly begin to assume there's a problem. It's taken me a long time to realise that very few people are like me in this respect. And the difference, I've come to believe, is that very few people think in terms of a sequence of events.

Somebody agrees to meet you at a specific time. In general, in my experience, they don't take into account other meetings, things running over, getting across town, finding an unfamiliar place, getting a parking place, all things which can blow their appointment with you completely out of the water. I once worked at a company where people would wander into a meeting, say on a Wednesday, and ask, 'Is this the Monday marketing meeting?' This was my sequence-of-events theory gone mad.

"Quite simply, without sequences of events, nothing gets done"

The overwhelming reason why sequences of events are so important is because, quite simply, without sequences of events, nothing gets done. Let's say you're buying a house and the estate agent phones you and says, 'The owners of the house like your offer – it looks like we have a deal on our hands.' 'Great,' you say. 'Yeah, it is great,' he says and the call finishes. Now, if that is all that happens, nothing will get done. Because maybe the estate agent is waiting for you to make the next move, and you think his is the next move, and so nothing actually happens. If, however, you ask, 'So what happens next?' or he volunteers,

'So, here's what has to happen now,' then this is the cue for you and him to build a sequence of events.

Maybe you would never let this happen if you were buying a house, or engaged in some other important personal event, but how many times have you gone to a meeting where the following has happened? There is a complete meeting of minds. Everybody is agreed that the issue needs to be resolved and the way forward is decided. Then everybody files out of the room. And hey, surprise surprise, nothing gets done. Nothing gets done because no sequence of events gets built. Or worse still, because nobody summarises (ideally in writing) the actions arising from the meeting, everybody builds their own version of the sequence of events.

In her book *The Seven Deadly Sins of Business*, Eileen Shapiro discusses the reasons that companies get into trouble. The first 'deadly sin' is that too many companies identify an aggressive goal or vision or targets, then pay scant attention to 'how' those targets/that goal/those visions will be achieved. She is saying precisely what we are saying. If there is no sequence of events, nothing gets done. As Bill Gates famously put it, 'Vision without execution is day dreaming.'

And then there's the issue of dealing with specialists. Doctors, lawyers and software people are probably the worst offenders, but many people do it. You know the kind of thing I mean – somebody takes the attitude that they know better than you and that you should just leave things to them. They talk (often condescendingly) to you in the technobabble of their particular discipline in the hope that it will baffle you into silence. If that doesn't work, and you actually question them, they continue to send over waves of technobabble to intimidate you into silence. Almost always too – particularly with lawyers and software people – there's a sense of, 'It'll take as long as it takes. Don't ask why – it just will.'

The truth is that doctors, lawyers and software people – indeed, all specialists – are as subject to the rule of sequences of events as the next person. With doctors, to hand your health or even your life over to someone like this is crazy. With lawyers, it is often your financial well-being that is at stake; and many of us these days are having to deal with software people. If you are in charge – which you are if you hire a doctor, hire a lawyer or are managing a software person – then among other things the onus is on them to tell you clearly and unambiguously what the sequence of events is.

"You are entitled to question the sequence of events"

Furthermore, you are entitled to question the sequence of events. This is particularly true of lawyers and software people. What happens next? What does what you just said mean? What does it translate into in simple language? Who is doing what? Why does it take this long? ('It just does' is not a good enough answer.) Why can't it be done quicker? What's the holdup? Explain to me in simple language who is doing what. What am I expected to do? Keep doing this until you get a clear picture in your mind of what is going on. Don't be afraid to make suggestions or offer improvements to the plan (i.e. the sequence of events). Once they get the hang of how the game is going to be played, they'll deliver a much better service for your (or your company's) money.

A different way of thinking about all of this is to say that sequences of events are our best shot at understanding what will happen in the future. Which is just a complicated way of saying that sequences of events are *plans*, or, to be slightly more precise, sequences of events are the foundations of plans. And good sequences of events are the foundations of good plans. How was some great undertaking, say D-Day, planned? Primarily because many many people built large, complicated, interconnected sequences of events.

If we know what we are trying to do (from Chapter 2) and can build sequences of events to do it, we are well on the way to getting lots of the things we want to do, done. The next question then is, what tools are there that can help us to build sequences of events? It turns out that there are six of them:

1. Plan at the beginning.

2. Do it in as much detail as possible.

3. Say what you mean.

4. Use knowledge and assumptions.

5. Use cause and effect.

6. Record what actually happens.

We discuss them in turn in the next section.

How to

Plan at the beginning

There are three ways in which sequences of events can get built. Unfortunately, two of them are no good. Even more unfortunately, it is these two that tend to be used most often!

The first way that sequences of events get built is by doing nothing at all. The sequence of events just sort of unfolds itself. Here's how that can happen. Charlie arrives at the office in the morning and says, 'Hmmm, what'll I do today?' He does something. Then he realises he needs something from somebody else, so he wanders down the corridor and says, 'Hey, Fred, do you have that other thing?' But maybe Fred says he won't have that until Friday and so Charlie shrugs and does something else and so the project unfolds with things just ... well, sort of happening.

"In your organisation today there are almost certainly projects that are being run like this"

Now clearly, nobody would consciously do this. But in your organisation today there are almost certainly projects that are being run like this. Typically, they're not being run like this because people are stupid or incompetent. They're being run like this because people don't have enough *time* available to run the project. If people are too busy, are trying to keep too many balls in the air, are multi-tasking so much that they don't have time available to run the project, then this is what will happen.

The second way that sequences of events get built is in real time. Here's what this is like. You arrive at the office in the morning and look at your to-do list. You start doing the first thing on the list but then somebody reminds you to come to the nine thirty meeting. During the meeting, somebody knocks on the door and says, 'Can I speak to you for a minute?' While you're speaking to them, your mobile phone rings so you answer that. Then your computer goes 'bing!' because an email has arrived. And then your land line rings ... You get the idea. You sort of ricochet through the day. Gotta go here, gotta go there, do that thing, talk to that guy ... You may be familiar with the 'f' word – 'firefighting'.

Firefighting is a term used to describe how you deal with crises or unexpected events. A firefight occurs when something you didn't anticipate occurs and you have to deal with it.

Sure, firefighting happens on projects. No matter how carefully they're planned, firefights are going to happen. But not everything that happens on a project is a firefight. Many things that happen on projects could have been predicted – if only you'd thought about them. Firefighting – the recipe for a short, unhappy life – is certainly not the way to build the sequence of events.

That leaves one other possibility when it comes to building the sequence of events. This is to do it right at the beginning – before you have made any commitments to any stakeholders, before you start hiring people or allocating jobs or burning up the budget, you should build as much of the sequence of events as you can. Firefights will still happen – but then you can save your energy for the things that are genuine firefights; as opposed to the things which would never have become firefights if only you had thought about them.

Do it in as much detail as possible

The next important thing to bear in mind is the level of detail in which the sequence of events is described. The D-Day people didn't just say:

1. Start.

2. Rustle up five divisions.

3. Ship them to Normandy.

4. Get them ashore.

5. The end.

While at its highest level the plan may have indeed looked like this, for it to have been in any way valid or usable it needed to be worked down to *as much detail as could possibly be imagined*. 'The devil is in the detail,' the old saw goes, and how true it is. It is only when we burrow down into the detail, it is only as we imagine the various events taking place, and how the result of one event is then the start point for the next event, that we can unearth all the potential obstacles that lie up ahead. While there are exceptions, for most of the situations we encounter these days, a level of detail where every job can be measured in the range of one to five days is what you need to be aiming for. Notice this means that, depending on the scale of the project, you may be required to go through a number of levels of detail before you get to the one to five day level.

Say what you mean

There's an exercise I do on my project management courses in which I ask people to estimate how long it will take to carry out a job called 'Review document', i.e. the review of a certain document. The document is about 15 pages long. Believe it or not, the answers I have received over the years have varied from half an hour up to *six months*.

Why the huge discrepancy? It's because it isn't at all clear what I mean by the word 'review'. Because suppose I mean one person reviewing the 15-page document. Then maybe half an hour is the right answer. If, on the other hand, 'review' means an individual review, followed by a meeting, followed by the document being updated, followed by a second review to sign the document off, followed by maybe a further review cycle by, say, senior management, then maybe the answer is closer to six months.

So when you write sequences of events, say exactly what you mean. 'Write it as though you were writing it for a six-year-old' is the advice I give my course attendees.

"Write it as though you were writing it for a six-year-old"

Use knowledge and assumptions

Of course, you may object and say, 'But I can't know all the events, I can't know all the detail.' And this is indeed true. So then the rule is simple. Where you have knowledge, use it. Where you don't, where you come up against something and you have no idea what comes next, make some assumption. For example, how did the Allies know what kind of opposition they would face on Omaha Beach? Answer is, they didn't – for sure. But they had some knowledge, based on intelligence, reconnaissance and so on. For the rest they made assumptions. And these assumptions enabled them to continue to chain together sequences of events.

Use cause and effect

This is just a fancy way of saying that jobs don't exist in isolation and that, as soon as you write down one job, it triggers other jobs. These in turn trigger other jobs and so the sequences of events get built. So all you have to do is write down the first job and then keep asking the question, 'What happens next?'

Record what actually happens

All the previous tools assumed you were starting from a blank sheet of paper. Often this is the case; the particular thing you are doing has not been done before and you are setting off into the great unknown. More often though, we are doing things that *have* been done before. (D-Day, for example, learned many lessons from the disastrous amphibious raid on Dieppe two years earlier.) Thus it should be possible to draw on other people's experience to build the sequence of events; our team may know things, or our peers, or somebody somewhere in the organisation.

Even if that is not the case, that shouldn't stop you from quickly building up your own bank of knowledge as your venture unfolds. When you build a sequence of events, see how what actually happens compares with the original sequence. For example, you thought something was going to take three days but it actually took twice that. The material captured in this way is like treasure in heaven.

The next time you come to plan something that is even remotely similar, you will find that you are able to use useful information from your databank. In addition, if you are asked to review other people's plans, you can compare what they are proposing with what is in your databank, and almost always draw useful conclusions. Finally, when someone (e.g. a boss or stakeholder) questions your estimates, if you can say something like, 'Well, the last five times we did this it took this long', this will add great authority to your plans.

These, then, are the six tools that enable us to build a sequence of events. It has to be said that many people never go to the trouble of building sequences of events. They feel it is too much effort (it isn't). Or they feel that they can't (they can). Or that the effort far outweighs the benefit (not true either).

Finally, just as a footnote, if your business is project management, you'll probably have deduced by now that a sequence of events is remarkably similar to what you would call a work breakdown structure or WBS.

Examples/Applications

Example 1 Planning a project

Using the tools just described it is possible to estimate and plan whole projects. So let's take what could be a real project and see just enough of this working that you get the gist of it.

Let's say that the project is to change some business process that we currently have. So right now, we do things a certain way, but we're going to change that to a new way of working. The change will involve changes not just to what people do but also to the computer system that they use. Let's use our tools to build a piece of the plan for this project, a step at a time.

Step 1 Figure out the jobs to be done

What might be the highest level of detail for a project like this? Okay, how about:

1. Figure out what changes have to be made (to processes, to the computer system).

2. Make the changes to the processes.

3. Make the changes to the computer system.

4. Document the new way of working.

5. Train everybody in the new way of working.

6. Test that everything works.

7. Go live.

Now let's take one of these big pieces and break it down into the detailed jobs. Let's take point 6, 'Test that everything works', on the basis that it's furthest away in time and so should be hardest to do.

'Test that everything works' can begin when big pieces 1–5 have been done. So let's use our tools. Big piece point 5 says that we've trained everybody in the new way of working. So what happens next? We have to figure out what we're going to test. And what happens next? We get some people to carry out the tests. And what happens next? They find errors. And what happens next? We fix the errors. And what happens next? They test again and find more errors.

You see how it goes. So here's what this might look like when we write it all down:

6   Test that everything works.

    6.1 Figure out what we're going to test.

    6.2 Get some people to carry out the tests and report errors.

    6.3 Fix the errors.

    6.4 Repeat 6.2 and 6.3 a number of times.

Okay, so the next question is, what does 'a number of times' actually mean? Well, clearly we don't know how many iterations of finding and fixing errors we're going to have to do. So what do we do? Hey, we make an assumption. And just for simplicity here and to keep the example manageable, let's assume three times. So:

6   Test that everything works.

    6.1 Figure out what we're going to test.

    6.2 Set up a test environment.

    6.3 Get some people to carry out the tests and report errors.

    6.4 Fix the errors.

    6.5 Repeat 6.3 and 6.4 three times.

Step 2 Figure out the work in those jobs

Now let's figure how much work is in each of these jobs:

    6.1 Figure out what we're going to test. This involves somebody writing some kind of test plan. Let's assume that 1 person can do this in 5 days. That's 5 PD (person-days).

6.2 Set up a test environment. Let's assume that 1 person can do this in 3 days. That's 3 PD.

6.3 Carry out the tests and report errors. Let's assume that 3 people are required to carry out the tests and it takes them 2 days each. That's 6 PD.

6.4 Fix the errors. Let's assume that we find 10 errors. Let's further assume that out of these 10, 1 is Big, 3 are Medium and the other 6 are Small. And finally, let's assume that it takes 3 days to fix a Big error, a day to fix a Medium and that a Small can be done in half a day. (Please be clear that I'm just making these numbers up. If they can be based on previous experience that's great, but otherwise you just make the best guess you can.) So then the total work involved in fixing the errors is $1 \times 3 + 3 \times 1 + 6 \times \frac{1}{2} = 9$ PD.

6.5 For the second test round, let's assume that we test everything again, not just the things that were wrong the first time and got fixed. (This is because we want to ensure that by fixing the things we fixed, we didn't introduce errors into things that worked right the first time.) So, a second 6 PD. Let's assume that the second time out we get a smaller number of errors – say, no Big, 1 Medium, 4 Small. This gives 3 PD ($1 \times 1 + 4 \times \frac{1}{2}$).

Finally, in the third test round, our 3 testers do 1 day of testing each and we assume that everything works perfectly and that there is no further fixing, i.e.:

	Testing	Fixing	Altogether
First test round	6	9	15
Second test round	6	3	9
Third test round	3	0	3
Totals	15	12	27

Step 3 Figure out dependencies and durations

Then let's add the dependencies – the cause and effect, the what depends on what (see table below).

Depends on	Jobs	Work (person-days)
	START	**0**
	1 Figure out what changes have to be made	
1	**2 Make the changes to the processes**	
2	**3 Make the changes to the computer system**	
2,3	**4 Document the new way of working**	
4	**5 Train everybody in the new way of working**	
5	**6 Test that everything works**	**35**
	6.1 Figure out what we're going to test	5
6.1	6.2 Set up a test environment	3
6.2	6.3 Carry out the tests and report errors (first round)	6
6.3	6.4 Fix the errors (first round)	9
6.4	6.5 Carry out the tests and report errors (second round)	6
6.5	6.6 Fix the errors (second round)	3
6.6	6.7 Carry out the tests and report errors (third round)	3
6	**7 Go live**	
7	**END**	

And now let's figure out how long things are going to take. (Note that 'how long' is sometimes also called 'duration'. Note too that 'how long' is different from 'how many days' work', i.e. the person-days that we calculated in the last step.)

6.1 Figure out what we're going to test. We said that this was 1 person for 5 days. Thus the duration is 5 days.

6.2 Set up a test environment. We said that 1 person can do this in 3 days. That's 3 days' duration.

6.3 Carry out the tests and report errors (round 1). We said 3 people for 2 days. Thus the duration is 2 days.

6.4 And so on to give us the plan like that shown in the table overleaf.

Step 4 Figure out the budget

And finally, let's do the budget for the jobs in point 6, 'Test that everything works'. To do this we just need to realise that:

- some jobs consist of a certain number of work days and nothing else. All we do for these is multiply the number of work days by a daily rate that we would get from Finance;

- some jobs consist of the preceding plus other costs – such as travel, equipment and so on. For these other costs, we can (a) ask a supplier, (b) look on the internet or (c) make an assumption;

- some jobs are subcontracted where we pay somebody a fee to do the work.

And there we have it – almost a plan for a piece of a project. To finish it off all we'd have to do is to add who's going to do what and we'd be in business.

Depends on	Jobs	Work (person-days)	Duration (days)
	START	**0**	
	1 Figure out what changes have to be made		
1	**2 Make the changes to the processes**		
2	**3 Make the changes to the computer system**		
2,3	**4 Document the new way of working**		
4	**5 Train everybody in the new way of working**		
5	**6 Test that everything works**	**35**	
	6.1 Figure out what we're going to test	5	5
6.1	6.2 Set up a test environment	3	3
6.2	6.3 Carry out the tests and report errors (first round)	6	2
6.3	6.4 Fix the errors (first round)	9	3
6.4	6.5 Carry out the tests and report errors (second round)	6	2
6.5	6.6 Fix the errors (second round)	3	1
6.6	6.7 Carry out the tests and report errors (third round)	3	1
6	**7 Go live**		
7	**END**		

Notice too that there's another example of building a plan at the beginning of this chapter. We did it when we planned the Disneyland Paris trip. It's all there – jobs, durations, assumptions, who's doing what, the works.

Example 2 Meetings again

Let's say, for example, you're going to a meeting. Are you just at the mercy of whatever pops up at the meeting or can you do a bit better than that? The question is rhetorical because of course you can do better than that. For starters, you can decide what result you want to get from the meeting (rule 2) and then you can figure out how you might get it (rule 3).

Let's say the meeting is with a client and it's a difficult topic – it's about rebuilding a relationship that's gone off the rails. Not that anything particularly disastrous happened, just that it was perhaps at times mishandled, left untended; incorrect perceptions were allowed to spring up and fester and, generally, the thing wasn't given professional tender loving care.

"What are we trying to get from the meeting?"

So you start by asking, 'What are we trying to get from the meeting?' An order? Hardly. Even if by some bizarre turn of fate they offered you one, you should almost (I said 'almost'!) be thinking in terms of declining it. Your emphasis today is on rebuilding the relationship. And on the basis that Rome wasn't built in a day, maybe you decide that the best you can hope to achieve today is to give them a feeling that you care. You want them to know, at the conclusion of the meeting, that you want to do business with them in the future and that you have value which you think you can add to their business. But you don't want it to be a sales pitch.

Let's say there are two of you going – you, because you have inherited the account, and your boss. You have asked for the meeting. The guys are giving you 20 minutes. (The detail is somewhat unimportant here except to illustrate things. What's important is how you have clearly set out what you do and don't hope to get from the meeting.) Now the sequence of events. You discuss it with your boss beforehand and settle on something like the following:

1. Your boss will open the meeting. He will thank them for taking the time out and explain that the purpose is to begin the process of rebuilding something which has been neglected. He will explain how you think you can still add value and how you hope to be a valuable supplier to them in the future. Then he will give them an opening to have a gripe.

2. You assume they will take the opportunity and that this will be the greater part of the meeting.

3. You agree that you will take their gripes on the chin, not trying to give excuses or correct them even if they're wrong. You may occasionally tell them of steps you have taken and things you have put in place to fix some of the problems they describe. Your boss will lead and you'll take notes.

4. You decide you'll allow the first three items to take at most 15 minutes so that you have a few minutes to close and get out within the 20 minutes they gave you.

5. Since every meeting should end with some kind of action – to keep the chain of events unbroken – you might mention to them that you plan to bid for the next piece of business that comes out (action on you) or tell them not to forget you next time they're looking for a blah supplier (action on them).

6. Finally, you'll thank them for their input, remind them of the value you can add, reiterate that you want to put the past behind you and move forward into what will be, it is hoped, a better relationship for both parties. Then you will say your goodbyes.

In terms of your goal, this should get you there. If it all goes horribly wrong, there's probably not much you can do except to get out with as much of your dignity intact as possible.

Again, the details are less important than the idea of using the two rules – figure out what you're trying to do and then put a sequence of events in place to do it.

Example 3 Dealing with lots of things/prioritising

You may be trying to do a bunch of things. If you haven't established a sequence of events for each one, it's quite likely you'll end up flitting from one to the other, never sure (a) if you're progressing things and (b) if you're progressing the right things.

Once you have a sequence of events for each of the things you're trying to do, all of this changes. Then each sequence of events is like a stack of jobs to be done. By taking the top item from each stack you progress that particular thing forward. If you take the top item from every stack, everything gets moved forward. Even more usefully, when new things come winging in from outfield, you can check them against those stacks you're working with and see if they are relevant to things going on in the stacks. If they are, you can deal with them. If not, you can put them to one side. (Thus the best way to deal with an inbox is as follows: screen it for anything that needs dealing with straight away, i.e. relevant to one of the stacks you have going, otherwise leave it in a pile to be cleared once a week, once a fortnight, once a month – the longer the interval the better, in my view.)

If, in addition to all of this, you are good at prioritising, you can restrict the number of things you concentrate on (and hence the number of stacks you have on the go) to the bare minimum that will make the biggest difference. (One suspects an 80/20 rule is operating here – do 20 per cent of the things and get 80 per cent of your job done.) To be good at prioritising, just do the following: look at all the things you have on the go and ask yourself the question, 'If I could only do one thing, what would it be?' Having answered it, take the remaining items and ask the question again. Do this until all items have been assigned a priority. Try to ensure that two items don't have the same priority, because then it's not really a priority, is it?

"Ask yourself the question, 'If I could only do one thing, what would it be?'"

Example 4 Speeding things up

Having a sequence of events for each of the things you are trying to do also means that you can accelerate them.

You know how it goes. There's something we're trying to do. It invariably involves other people. We do our bit, we give it to them and there it often hangs in some form of suspended animation.

But if we have a stack of events, we can look further down the stack rather than just at the top item and see other stuff that could be done to move the thing forward. Thus while we're waiting for the other thing to happen we can still make progress. Often too this has the nice side effect of putting pressure on the laggards to complete their stuff.

Example 5 Discussions that lead nowhere

Have you ever had one of those discussions that leads nowhere? I'm sure you know the kind of thing I mean. You and a colleague (or maybe several of them) have a discussion where you are entirely in agreement about something. 'Somebody really ought to do something' seems to be the unspoken subtext. However, at the end of the discussion, everyone walks away and nothing happens. (Actually, in my experience, whole meetings can often be conducted like this.)

Knowing that there is always a sequence of events can stop this from happening. If there is agreement on some issue, then for anything to happen, a sequence of events must flow from that agreement. Pointing this out and putting even one or two jobs in train (i.e. putting actions on people) ensures that whatever great idea was hatched during the discussion is not forgotten, but rather is acted upon.

AND SO, WHAT SHOULD YOU DO?

1. Keep a list of the things you're trying to do.

2. Update it regularly – every day, every week, whatever works for you.

3. Use rule 2 to understand new things as they come along. Then use the tools we have described in the 'How to' section of this chapter to build sequences of events. Keep sequences of events in stacks and work the stacks as we have described.

4. Always look for action lists after meetings, phone calls and so on.

5. Make bread in parallel with doing something else. Bread making is a classic example of a sequence of events. Making bread while doing one or more other things is a great way of practising doing many things at once, i.e. managing sequences of events.

6. Always try to have a plan (sequence of events) for a meeting, for a working day, for a project. It'll go so much more smoothly as a result.

4

Chapter

Things don't get done if people don't do them

This chapter makes the rather obvious point that things won't be done if people don't do them. In particular, things won't get done if people don't have the time to do them.

Questions

Take a minute to answer these two questions:

1. You've been called in to 'rescue' of a project or venture. There is a plan that is actually current. The plan has a well-defined goal and a comprehensive list of jobs (sequence of events). In looking at the plan you find that lots of the jobs have phrases such as 'New hire', 'TBD', 'A N Other' against them, i.e. generic names rather than real people's names. Is this the main reason why the venture went wrong?

2. You're ready to begin a new venture with the merry band of brothers (and sisters) that you've chosen, inherited or otherwise acquired. Of the following, which is most likely to sink your venture?

    (a) Poor salaries.

    (b) Poor working conditions.

    (c) Not playing to people's strengths.

    (d) Poor management by you.

The rule

Once you've figured out what it is you're trying to do (rule 2, know what you're trying to do) and what needs to happen to get it done (rule 3, there is always a sequence of events), the next thing is to get the things done. That is what this chapter is all about. But first a story.

A few years ago, my ex-wife's nephew spent a few weeks in our company on work experience from school. Shortly after he started with us, I was chatting with him and he asked, 'What exactly do you do here anyway?' I explained that we were a project management company that worked with high-tech and knowledge industries. We did training, we did consulting, we ran projects for clients. He asked about the training courses. 'What kinds of things do you teach them?' 'Oh,' I said, 'for example, we teach that if you have a big job to do, you break it up into lots of smaller jobs.' 'So what else?' he asked. 'Well, we teach them that jobs don't get done if people don't do them.' At this he smiled. 'You teach this to adults?' he asked. I nodded. 'Is it expensive?' he asked. 'It's not cheap,' I replied. His smile broadened and he began to shake his head. 'I'd better go back to work,' he said.

"Jobs *don't* get done if people don't do them"

It's so sickeningly obvious, and yet jobs *don't* get done if people don't do them, and if enough jobs don't get done, then things go awry, sometimes badly so. In general, people don't maliciously set out not to do things. But there are a variety of reasons why it can happen. The most obvious ones are:

- confusion – they didn't know they were meant to do something or precisely what it was they were meant to do;

- over-commitment – they knew they were meant to do it but they didn't have the time;

- inability – they didn't have the expertise, experience or training to do the job.

So if we are to address the problem of people not doing certain things, our tools must tackle these three killers. We introduce the tools in the next section. They are:

- Making sure every job has somebody to do it. This should deal with individual confusion.

- Dance cards – to deal, first of all, with over-commitment but also with confusion within an organisation.

- Maximising the strengths of the team. This should deal with inability.

And the answers to the questions at the head of the chapter? Question 1 – if the goal was stable (rule 2) and the sequence of events was well thought out (rule 3), then you can depend on it. Stands to reason, doesn't it? If things were meant to be done and they weren't, then of course it's going to go pear-shaped.

Question 2 – yep, it's (c). Play to people's weaknesses and it'll go down the tubes faster than you can say 'Human Resources issue'.

How to

Make sure every job has somebody to do it

Our first tool is a pretty straightforward one. We just want to make sure that at the end of a meeting, a phone call, at the start of a project or venture, we know who has to do what. I'll fully accept that at the beginning of a venture we may not know who's going to work on what. They may not have been identified, assigned or hired. So it is perfectly valid for us to have certain jobs in our sequences of events where nobody has been identified to do them. Then it's fine if we put in 'generic' names such as 'Marketing person' or 'Engineer' or 'Designer', or even the dreaded 'TBDs' and 'New hires' and 'A N Others'.

But *some time before that job is due to happen*, there had better be a warm, living, loving human being in place who is actually going to get the job done.

Dance cards

You may not have necessarily thought of things in this way before, but much of life is a problem in supply and demand. Money. We don't have enough money (supply) to do all the things we'd like to do (demand). Or we have a business and it is successful – revenue (supply) exceeds costs (demand). Or, heaven forbid, our business is unsuccessful because revenue (supply) is less than costs (demand). Or, thinking about resources, we (as a department, division, organisation, company) are trying to do too much with too few people or too little equipment. Or, thinking in terms of time, there never seem to be enough hours in the day (supply) to do all the things we want to do, have to do or have committed to do (demand).

"Much of life is a problem in supply and demand"

A dance card is a way of investigating *time* from a supply and demand point of view. Just to get it out of the way, the term 'dance card' is a reference to those more genteel days when ladies went to dances and had a dance card showing the (fixed number of) dances that were available that night. Then, if a gentleman wanted to dance with them, he wrote his name against a particular dance – a waltz or a tango or whatever. Thus that time slot was booked, if you want to think of it that way, and so could not be booked by anybody else.

I hope you can see the analogy. You have a certain amount of time (or time slots) available every day, every week, every month, every year. In work, at home or wherever, certain slots get booked by other people – your boss, your customer, people who work for you, your children, your wife, husband, boyfriend, girlfriend and so on. Given that, in general, there will be more demand on your time than you will be able to satisfy, how can you ensure that you put time into the right things? The dance card, which we will describe shortly, is a tool for doing just that. It also has other uses, but let's see first what a dance card looks like (see Table 4.1 overleaf).

I'm sure you can see that it looks suspiciously like it was made using a spreadsheet. The leftmost column lists all the things in which the dance card's owner is involved. The next two columns indicate how much work is estimated to go into these things over the period under investigation. Days per month (dpm), days per week (dpw), hours per day or just plain days are all good ways of estimating how much work needs to be done. The remaining columns show how this work will be spread out over the period under investigation – in this case, eight months. There are two other items of interest. The top row shows how many days are available per month and also the total number of days available (160) over the period. (Note that rather than trying to allow for the different numbers of working days in different countries, we have assumed that every month consists of 20 days. You could adjust this up or down for your

Table 4.1 A dance card

Total days available:	160		20	20	20	20	20	20	20	20
# Project	Basis	Total	Nov	Dec	Jan	Feb	Mar	Apr	May	Jun
1 Project Abel	25 days	25	2.5	2.5	2.5	3.5	3.5	3.5	3.5	3.5
2 Project Baker	25 days	25	2.5	2.5	2.5	3.5	3.5	3.5	3.5	3.5
3 Project Charlie	2 dpm	16	2	2	2	2	2	2	2	2
4 Project Dog	1 dpw	40	5	5	5	5	5	5	5	5
5 Email	8 dpm	64	8	8	8	8	8	8	8	8
6 Training other people	1 dpm	8	1	1	1	1	1	1	1	1
7 Recruitment	1 dpm	8	1	1	1	1	1	1	1	1
8 Project Easy	10 days	10	2	2	1	1	1	1	1	1
9 Holidays	5 days	5		5						
10 Meetings	2.5 dpw	80	10	10	10	10	10	10	10	10
11 Training courses	2 days	2	0.5	0.5	1					
12 Trips	2 days	2			2					
13 Conference calls	0.5 dpm	4	0.5	0.5	0.5	0.5	0.5	0.5	0.5	0.5
Total days work to do:		289	35.0	40.0	36.5	35.5	35.5	35.5	35.5	35.5

own situation. For example, in Europe, December is definitely not 20 working days in most companies.) The other item of interest is the total of all the work this dance card owner has to do – in this example, 289 days.

Now here the owner has some problems to address – that's if you'd call having twice as much work to do as time available to do it a problem, which I believe I would. We will look at how one might address such a problem in Example 1 later in the chapter. I hope, though, you can see that the dance card is a good tool for understanding the sources of over-commitment.

Maximise the strengths of the team

One of the most foolish assumptions we could make would be to assume that just because we've got our sequence of events and we've given each job to some member of our motley crew, it's all going to happen. Apart from the reasons already identified – confusion or over-commitment – there is the question of expertise and ability. Looking at it somewhat more broadly or holistically, we can think of it like this: given that everybody has strengths and weaknesses, how can we ensure that we use as many of the strengths as possible and reduce as much as possible the effects of the weaknesses?

"How can we ensure that we use as many of the strengths as possible?"

Whole rainforests have been destroyed to provide the paper for the books, MBA theses and all the rest of the things that have been written in relation to this. In keeping with our philosophy of finding a simple solution (rule 1, many things are simple), however, the following is a method that I have used and found to be both useful and effective.

For each job allocated to a person, rate that allocation as in column two in the table below.

Name	Description	Management style
1 Superstar	The person likes to do that particular job, has all the necessary skills and will almost certainly deliver.	Leave them to get on with it with minimal sticking your nose in.
2 Solid citizen	The person is happy enough to do the job and knows how to do it. Maybe they don't get particularly fired up about doing it, but there's a pretty good chance they'll deliver.	Don't get too much in their way, but neither assume it's all just going to happen.
3 Dodgy	For whatever reason – lack of motivation, lack of expertise, lack of time – there's a good chance this one isn't going to happen.	Establish as quickly as you can – by giving them a few jobs from the sequence of events and seeing the result – whether it's going to happen or not. If it is, it becomes a 2 – solid citizen; if not, it becomes a 5 – goner.
4 Trainee	They're new to whatever it is. They're going to need hand-holding, nurturing, mentoring, coaching, formal training, micro-management before you can be confident they'll deliver.	Do all of what we said in the previous list to ensure you make them into at least a 2 – solid citizen.
5 Goner	It isn't going to happen. You need to find some other way of getting this job done.	You need to deal with the person. Your choices are anything on the spectrum from firing to rehabilitation.

Now, we can make a few observations about this scheme. The first is, how do we know that a person falls into a particular category if we've never worked with them before? Simple. Give them a few jobs from the sequence of events and see how they do. After two or three deliveries or non-deliveries, we'll have a much clearer idea.

Next, who should decide who falls into a particular category? Two possibilities. You can decide and act accordingly. Alternatively – and this is better, but maybe harder to do – you and the person can rate their capabilities on particular jobs. Then you compare notes and you (both) see where you might have not estimated the person's ability to deliver correctly.

Finally, what do the classifications mean for you? The main thing is that you will manage the different situations differently. For example, you wouldn't manage a superstar the same way you would a trainee. In fact, column three shows the leadership or management styles that would seem most appropriate in the different situations.

Examples/Applications

Example 1 Common-sense time management

There was a theory doing the rounds about 20 or so years ago that said that in a few years' time we'd have all this leisure time that we wouldn't know what to do with. The notion was that with all the various labour-saving devices around (especially computers and computer-driven devices), a lot of our day-to-day drudgery would be taken away from us. The concern then was about 'educating people for leisure'. Funnily enough, you don't hear much about that any more. And try telling it to an urban couple who get up at some ungodly hour, wash, feed, ferry children to a number of different schools or crèches, join the traffic jam to work, work an eight-hour day (if they're lucky) and then do it all in reverse that evening.

Just as an aside, it seems to me that there was a basic flaw in this and a number of other assumptions made about modern society. Rule 1, many things are simple, enables us to spot this flaw without too much difficulty. It is best illustrated by an example. You may remember the notion of the 'paperless office' that was fashionable during the 1980s. The idea was that you would give people computers with plenty of disk storage, high-speed printers, copiers, electronic links and the result would be the disappearance of filing cabinets and paper. Everything would be available online. Now thinking simply about this, the notion is ludicrous. If you give people the ability (using computers, networks, printers and copiers) to generate and pass around large amounts of paper, what will they do? In all probability, they'll generate and pass around large amounts of paper. (We can see the same effect with traffic. If you give people the ability to do a lot more driving by building lots of cars and more roadways, what will they do? Hey, they'll drive more cars and fill more roadways.)

So, returning to the notion of time management and leisure time, if you give people the ability to communicate more or less instantaneously, what will happen? People will use that ability to try to run their jobs or their businesses faster. They will try to get more done more quickly. So will this have a relaxing effect? Well, you could hardly call getting more done more quickly a recipe for relaxation, could you?

Anyway, back to the main point. Common-sense time management. In your career you may have done time management courses or read time management books. Unless they were completely execrable you may have picked up some good ideas from them. But I'd be prepared to bet that you still don't feel you've solved your time management problem. There's a simple reason for this and it's to be found in rule 4. You haven't solved your time management problem because you have too much to do and not enough time to do it. To put it another way, your jobs aren't getting done because there isn't enough of *you* to do them. And, in general then, this is the problem with most time management books/courses/'systems' – they don't solve the right problem. Sure, they'll make you more efficient and enable you to make better use of your time. But that's not the problem you really want to solve. The problem you really want to solve is the one of too much to do and not enough time to do it.

"We must learn *not* to do things"

Is there a solution to this problem? Yes, there is. In keeping with rule 1, it is a very simple one. The solution to the problem of too much to do and not enough time to do it is that we must learn *not* to do things. If this is not a skill you have learned in your career to date, then it's time that you did. There are three things you need to learn and practise.

Learn and practise saying 'no' nicely

Do this now. Sit down by yourself or with a friend or colleague and make a list of a dozen ways to say 'no' nicely. You'll find it's not difficult. (If you're too lazy to do this, you could also Google 'ways to say "no" nicely'.) Now take some of these techniques and try them out. In work.

At home. Try this for a week. I'm not saying that you necessarily have to say 'no' nicely to everything that comes your way – though you could. Just practise this essential skill of being able to turn some things away. What will you have achieved if you do this? Well, you'll have found a way to reduce the pile of stuff that needs to be done. Is this a good thing? You bet – because there is now less stuff to be done in the time available to do it. Okay, what next?

"Practise being able to turn some things away"

Learn and practise prioritising viciously

Firstly there's prioritising. We saw it in Chapter 3. We take a list, ask the question, 'If I could only do one thing what would it be?' and this becomes our number 1 priority. Then we take the remaining list, ask the question again. This becomes number 2. We keep doing this until our list is prioritised. Prioritising viciously takes this a stage further because we cut the list where – as determined by your dance card – supply equals demand. Another way to think about this is that some things on our list are *wildly* important – and some stuff … well, just isn't. So we invest our time in the things that are wildly important and we say 'no' nicely to the things that aren't.

Learn and practise planning

For those things that you have to do, you want to make sure they get done with the least amount of firefighting and nasty surprises. That's where planning comes in. We saw it in Chapter 3.

So in summary then, how do you solve the problem of too much to do and not enough time to do it?

1. Identify what's *wildly* important in your job (or life) and what isn't.

2. Say 'no' nicely to anything that isn't.

3. For the things that are wildly important, plan them and then work the plans. From personal experience I can tell you that if you were to do this, really, really do this, you would be staggered at how much you would get done and how much time you'd find opening up to you.

Example 2 Aligning goals or objectives

One of the problems that occurs a lot in business is when you have, say, a bunch of people working for you (in a project or in a department, for example) and what they do is not what you expect. This can be bad for a couple of reasons. First of all, clearly, you didn't get to where you expected to be. Second, and often more importantly, you don't find this out until much too late.

A lot of ways have been devised to try to address this situation – management by objectives, sometimes involving almost lawyer-like definition of objectives, balanced score cards, key performance indicators and so on. In my experience, dance cards represent a far better way to go about this. Here's how you do it:

1. Get each of the people who work for you to do a dance card to cover the period you're interested in.

2. Now go through the dance card with each person in turn, line by line.

3. Understand what they're intending to do over the period.

4. Look at the supply and demand and see how realistic the proposal is. (Hint: If they're as overloaded as shown in Table 4.1, for example, there's a fair chance that the things they're proposing to do won't happen. While there's no fun in finding this out, better to do so now than down the line.)

5. Correct any things that don't line up with your expectations so that you get a final dance card agreed by both parties that has a reasonable supply–demand balance.

6. Now let them loose, and you can be much more confident that their contribution to your success will be the one you wanted.

Example 3 Ensuring that your organisation delivers on its commitments

Do you have any of the following problems?

- You work in the product development or service delivery parts of your organisation. From your point of view it seems as if the people who are responsible for promising/committing things to customers always make unreasonable promises.

- You are a sales or marketing person or a person responsible for ensuring that promised customer service levels are achieved. It seems like the product development or service delivery people in your organisation never come through on the commitments you have made. This seems to be true even when (a) you feel you have made eminently reasonable promises and (b) you may have even gone to the trouble of checking with the appropriate people – 'Are you absolutely sure I can feel confident in promising this?'

- You are the head of an organisation of the types described above. You have a feeling that you are not getting enough 'bang for the buck', that somehow – although you can't quite see how – your organisation is inefficient. Or even – your darkest fear – inept; that it doesn't really know what it's about. You've tried lots of things – training, changes in management structure or personnel, quality improvement drives and pro-grammes – but the basic problem remains.

- You are anyone in the organisation and you find yourself working harder and harder and every day becoming more and more stressed.

"If you answered 'yes', put more simply, it means that you may be trying to do too much with too little"

If you answered 'yes' to any of the above questions, your problem may be the following. To put it in a fancy way, it could be that your organisation-wide demand exceeds supply. Put more simply, it means that you may be trying to do too much with too little. 'What's new?' I hear you say. I can understand why you might say that. Most organisations do. Indeed, there is an argument that says it's a good thing to do; that all organisations should strive such that their reach exceeds their grasp. For example, in a *Fortune* article entitled 'Reinvent your company', the author Gary Hamel says that the first rule for 'designing a culture that inspires innovation' is to 'set unreasonable expectations'. He quotes a GE Capital executive as saying: 'It is expected that we will grow earnings 20 per cent per year or more. When you have objectives that are that outlandish, it forces you to think very differently about your opportunities.'

Now I have no problem with any of this. Ambitious targets? Sure. Thinking innovatively about achieving them? Absolutely. But not at the expense of losing the plot. And certainly not by trying to pretend that our fourth rule of common sense, things don't get done if people don't do them, somehow doesn't apply to you. I'll state it as bluntly as I can: if your organisation is trying to do more work than there are people available to do it, you will end up not doing all of the things that need to be done. And depending on the shortfall between demand (work to be done) and supply (people available to do it), you may end up missing your targets by a little bit or by a mile.

"The tendency is more towards the latter end of the spectrum"

In my experience, the tendency is more towards the latter end of the spectrum. Organisations which have a supply–demand discrepancy usually have a *huge* supply–demand discrepancy. This is particularly true of fast-growth, high-tech organisations – especially if they have large amounts of somebody else's money paying for their endeavours.

So what should you do? It's simple, really. We've seen the approach already in this chapter. Figure out as an organisation how much demand there is (work to be done), figure out how much supply there is (people to do the work), prioritise the list, then make the cut. Forget about all those notions of extended overtime or 'stretch' targets (where 'stretch' generally equals 'impossible' or 'insane').

They quite simply don't work on any kind of sustainable basis. Table 4.2 lists a hypothetical (product development, in this case) organisation's projects together with the estimated amount of work in each project. Let's assume that they are looking at a 12-month period.

Now let's assume that the same organisation has a total of 1,892 person-weeks available to it over the same period.

Table 4.2 A hypothetical organisation's projects and estimated amount of work

Project	Work or Effort	
1 Project Abel	8	person-weeks
2 Project Baker	541	person-weeks
3 Project Charlie	48	person-weeks
4 Project Dog	440	person-weeks
5 Project Easy	368	person-weeks
6 Project Foxtrot	135	person-weeks
7 Project Golf	976	person-weeks
8 Project Hotel	1,032	person-weeks
9 Project India	256	person-weeks
10 Support of existing products (estimate based on so many weeks per product)	392	person-weeks
11 R & D (estimate based on so many people for so many weeks)	176	person-weeks
12 Training (estimate based on so much training per person)	96	person-weeks
Sub-total	4,468	person-weeks
Project management effort @ 10%	447	person-weeks
Contingency @15%	670	person-weeks
TOTAL	**5,585**	**person-weeks**

This takes into account people already on the payroll, plus those who will be hired during the same period. I think you can see that this organisation has a BIG problem. I hope that you can see that if you worked in such an organisation, all the scenarios I described at the beginning of this example would be happening.

To fix this problem, as the organisation must, it must 'make the cut' at the point at which supply matches demand. This will entail the following:

- continuing (presumably) to include items 10 Support, 11 R & D and 12 Training among those things which have to be done;

- continuing to add in the Project management and Contingency overheads;

- deciding which of the remaining projects it intends to do, so that the total of the projects plus Support, R & D, Training, Project management and Contingency doesn't exceed 1,892 person-weeks.

Will this be a pleasant exercise? No, I don't think so. When they realise all of the things that aren't going to get done, I suspect it will be distinctly unpleasant. Do they have to do it? Yes, I would argue that they do. What will happen to them if they don't do it? If this organisation (which is maybe not as hypothetical or as rare as you would have hoped) doesn't consciously and explicitly decide what it wants to do, chance will decide for it. And if you think that's a good way for an organisation to conduct its business and go about achieving its goals, there's not a lot I can add.

Just to add one small footnote to this example: you'll notice that we implicitly assumed that we were dealing with one sort of person or skill level. A person-week of any product developer's time was equivalent to that of any other product developer, and we were able to count them all up in one big bucket. In solving organisations' supply–demand problems we first need to solve the problem at this level. Then, when we have done that, we can move to a next level down where we look at how much of particular sets of skills we need. For example, again in a product development organisation, we might have to consider how many designers, developers, testers and so on we might need.

Example 4 Coping with interruptions

Have you ever thought how uncomplicated your working life would be if there were no interruptions? You'd plan your week out, establishing exactly what needed to get done, there would be ample time for everything, and you would travel home on Friday evening with a glow of self-satisfaction and a song in your heart.

"Your beautifully crafted plan can end up battered by surprises, interruptions and firefights"

Sadly, the world isn't like that, and your beautifully crafted plan for the week can end up so battered by surprises, interruptions and firefights that you travel home on Friday wondering how it could possibly be Friday already and where the week has gone.

It may surprise you to learn that you already know the cure for this. It's what I think of as the 'hot date' scenario. It goes like this. Imagine that on a particular day you had a hot date. How would you organise your day in these circumstances? Isn't it true that you would plan your day as accurately as you could, allowing strict time slots to get done each thing that needed to be done? But not only this, you would also do something else. Knowing how easy it is for somebody to spring surprises on you or interrupt you, you would actually allow time for this. Let's say you had to leave the office no later than five to make your hot date. Then you wouldn't plan to be finished by five. No, no, no. That would be much too risky. Instead, you would plan to be finished by four o'clock, then you could either leave at that point, or the extra hour would be there to save your bacon if something came up.

Now, even though we know this, it is not something we do every day. Indeed, we have a tendency to do completely the opposite. Even though we know from bitter experience that every day there are interruptions, we behave as if today – for some bizarre reason – there will be no interruptions at all. Moreover, we are surprised and unhappy when these interruptions then happen, even though all logic tells us that they were bound to happen.

So to deal with interruptions, the common-sense thing to do is to apply the 'hot date' scenario every day. Here's a simple and powerful way to do it:

1. Record, for a given week, the amount of time each day that you put into dealing with interruptions.

2. From this get a daily average.

3. This is the amount of time you should put into every day when you are planning your day.

Here's an illustration. Let's say that for a particular week, you record the following by way of time spent servicing interruptions:

Day	Monday	Tuesday	Wednesday	Thursday	Friday
Time spent (in hours)	2	8	0.5	1.5	3

Thus the daily average is three hours $((2 + 8 + 0.5 + 1.5 + 3)/5)$. Therefore, on the basis of this evidence, you are likely to spend three hours per day servicing interruptions. By factoring this into your time planning (you could do it on a dance card, for example), you can ensure that the day's interruptions don't blow away the things you really have to get done. A day like the Tuesday illustrated will still leave your day in tatters, but that's a darn sight better than having every day ending in tatters.

Example 5 Managing in recessionary times

Read this quote:

'Colgate Palmolive has a remarkable record of improving productivity, as reflected in gross margin, virtually every year for the past 15 years, even during the last recession. The process is ingrained, and it pays off impressively: in the brutally competitive, slow-growing business of household products, Colgate's stock has risen an average of 28 per cent annually over the past five years.'

The article from which this is taken makes the point that during a slowdown or recession, productivity typically goes through the floor. It goes on to say that you need to stop this from happening and, in fact, to cause the opposite to happen. Not only does this see you through the downturn, but it also puts you in a stronger position when things turn up.

No matter what business you are in, avoiding waste is one of the ways to improve productivity. Examples 1, 2 and 3 all provide powerful ways of avoiding waste. And ensuring we spend our (limited and precious) time on the right things.

"Avoiding waste is one of the ways to improve productivity"

AND SO, WHAT SHOULD YOU DO?

1. Keep a list of all the projects/ventures/endeavours/ undertakings for which you are responsible.

2. Make sure that after every meeting or phone call, and for every project/venture/endeavour/undertaking, there is a sequence of events (rule 3, there is always a sequence of events). For each job in the sequence, ensure that there is somebody available to do it when the time comes.

3. Maximise the strengths of the people you are working with. (Not necessarily just subordinates. Exactly the same idea will work with bosses, customers, peers or anybody else.)

4. Keep a dance card and use it to get a life if you don't already have one, using the ideas we described in Example 1.

5. Teach dance cards to those who work for you. Then use the dance cards to align their objectives with yours.

6. You can do the same with your peers. This will show you whether what all of you are planning to do tallies in any way with what your management expect of you and what they have committed your organisation to doing.

7. Do the organisation-wide supply–demand calculations for your organisation. Then make the cut.

8. Build time for interruptions into your day.

Chapter

5

Things rarely turn out as expected

Despite our best efforts, there will always be surprises. This chapter talks about minimising the number and effect of surprises.

Questions

True or false?

1. It's okay to hide contingency in a plan if that's the only way you can ensure it stays in.

2. Risks are threats to your project or venture. In assessing a particular risk, one of the main factors to consider is the likelihood of the risk happening.

3. In assessing a particular risk, one of the main factors to consider is the impact that risk will have if it should happen.

The rule

'Life is full of surprises.' There perhaps isn't a week goes by that we don't find ourselves either saying this or being reminded of how true it is. In a sense, a lot of the things we've talked about so far – rule 2, know what you're trying to do; 3, there is always a sequence of events; 4, things don't get done if people don't do them – have been about trying to reduce the likelihood of these surprises happening. You can think of dance cards as a way of looking into the future and searching for surprises.

Despite our best efforts, however, there will always be surprises out there waiting for us. 'If you don't actively attack the risks [on your project],' software authority Tom Gilb has written, 'the risks will actively attack you.' Sometimes I think we are like people walking through minefields. The tools we have described give us partial maps of the minefield, but we know that these maps are incomplete and that unknown mines still lie there waiting for us.

"This tool is the equivalent of wearing body armour as we pass through the minefield"

To deal with these mines, we need some tools, and we will describe two. The first is the use of contingency or padding or margin for error. This tool is the equivalent of wearing body armour as we pass through the minefield. We know the mines are there, we assume that it is going to be impossible to avoid stepping on some of them, so some of them will definitely explode. What we want to ensure, then, is that the explosions don't kill us. This is not a stupid approach. Not dying is a laudable and worthwhile aim! Contingency is a reactive thing. When a surprise occurs, the contingency (we hope) enables us to deal with it.

However, we can also do a smarter thing. We can look out over the minefield and identify suspicious looking bumps in the ground or signs of digging and say that there is a fair likelihood that there is a mine in a certain place. Then, as we progress through the minefield, we can try to manage our progress as best we can to get past those particular mines. These mines may still go off – and then the contingency is there to save our bacon. Not only that, but we may also have taken specific additional measures to deal with specific mines. And if the mines don't go off, then so much the better – our efforts will be repaid many times over in terms of the number of 'firefights' we don't have to fight. This latter approach is called risk management.

These two tools – the use of contingency and risk management – are described in the next section. And as for the questions at the top of the chapter – you should have answered true to all three of them. Read on if you're in any doubt.

How to

Contingency

It's possible to make this whole discussion reasonably complicated. Bearing in mind rule 1, many things are simple, let's see if we can avoid doing that. Therefore, rather than trying to get into an exhaustive discussion of contingency, let's converge quickly on a few simple ideas.

The first is, as we have said already, it's mandatory. It's not that you'll only have it on your more cushy undertakings and jettison it on those that are down to the wire, you must have it on every venture.

In mature industries, such as construction, manufacturing or film-making, contingency is a fact of life, the same way that raw materials or labour rates are facts of life. Unfortunately, the same cannot be said for a lot of the high-tech or knowledge industries that are floating around at the moment. Here contingency tends to be viewed with the same kind of suspicion and loathing normally afforded to a dog turd on somebody's shoe. Suspicion because somehow it's felt that the people asking for the contingency are going to use it to take a paid holiday. Loathing because it's seen as a way for people to take the easy way out, to 'remove the creative tension', to make things comfortable for themselves, to be cowards, to be sissies.

As a result of this bizarre view, the general tendency in such industries is to remove contingency whenever it's sighted. Given that we have already said that you have got to have contingency in the plan, you need to be aware of this tendency and counteract it when it arises. There are two ways to do this:

1. either put contingency explicitly into the plan and stop anyone from taking it out; or

2. hide it in the plan so that they can't find it.

There's actually a third option, which is to put the contingency in explicitly and let them take it out. Then they have the satisfaction of taking it out and you still have it in. And, of course, if you managed to stop them from taking it out, you would have twice as much and you wouldn't hear any arguments from me on that score.

Finally, how do you do it? Well, you can pad out the estimates, say, of budgets (i.e. make the budget bigger than you think you'll need) or resources needed (say you'll need more than you actually need or say you want to hold on to them for longer) or time needed (i.e. add extra time on to the project). There are some other ideas on this in the 'Examples/Applications' section later in the chapter.

Risk management

While there are lots of complicated approaches to risk management, here's a simple one that gets the job done. First it identifies the issues, then it gives us a way of dealing with them over the life of the venture.

To manage risks we need to know a few things about them:

- which risks are likely to affect our undertaking;

- the likelihood of each of those risks happening;

- the impact of each of those risks happening;

- a calculation of our exposure to each risk so that we can deal with the major exposures;

- action(s) we can take to reduce our exposures;

- indicators, which will enable us to see if a particular risk has begun to materialise.

We will use Table 5.1 (overleaf) to record all of this. Using this table will enable us to see what the main risks are on our venture (risks with exposure 9 and 6 will be the ones we focus on). Then, on an ongoing basis, we can update Table 5.1 to give us our 'top 10 risks' list. Focusing regularly (say, weekly) on these will ensure that we stay on top of the scary things as our venture unfolds.

"Risk analysis is best done by the people who are going to have to carry out that project"

Just as with estimating a project, risk analysis is best done by the people who are going to have to carry out that project. So get them together. Ask them to brainstorm all of the things they can think of that could go wrong on the project. (Notice that once you have done this once, you have a set of risks that can be your start point when you come to do risk analysis on any future projects.) Write these risks in the first column of your risk analysis form (Table 5.1). Now get the team to grade the risks according to their Likelihood – these go in the second column.

Then their Impact – into the third column. The Exposure column will then show you the major risks to the project.

Table 5.1 Risk management form

Risk	Likelihood	Impact	Exposure	Actions	Indicators
	1 = Low 2 = Medium 3 = High	1 = Low 2 = Medium 3 = High	Likelihood multiplied by Impact (a number between 1 and 9)		

Now focus on these. What would be the signs that these threats to your project were beginning to happen? Write these in the rightmost column. Finally, what actions can you take to deal with these risks? These go into the Actions column. Example 4 shows a complete risk analysis.

Examples/Applications

Example 1 Incremental delivery

Some projects can be thought of as 'all or nothing' projects. Either everything has to be delivered/work – or it doesn't. The big bang. The Y2K problem or the changeover (for those countries that did it) to the Euro are examples of such projects. But such projects are inherently high risk, because if the big day comes and nothing works, then you're sunk.

So to avoid this situation, see if you can roll out the project in a series of deliveries or increments. If you have to deploy something in seven locations, for example, don't try to do all seven of them together. Do one first. Learn from it. Make your mistakes. Then maybe do two more and then, finally, the remainder. Or think in terms of have-to-have and nice-to-have. Give them the have-to-haves first and then roll out the nice-to-haves after that. I hope you can see it's a way of putting contingency in your plan. And it's a way that stakeholders like. Stakeholders hate the big bang – it scares them.

"Think in terms of have-to-have and nice-to-have"

Here's an interesting example of doing this that I came across recently. A woman on one of my courses worked for an organisation that set up women's refuges. Her job was to set up three in a certain area. Her initial idea was to run the three projects to set up the three refuges in parallel. They would run together and finish at the same time. But she quickly realised that one of the biggest threats to all this was – as it is for many not-for-profit organisations – a budget cut. What if the funding was cut as she was part way through the three projects? So what she decided to do instead was to run one project and try to get it over the line. She would learn from this one and then she would run the other two in parallel. Even if the funding was cut, she had the possibility of ending up with something rather than nothing.

Example 2 Under-promise and over-deliver

If you can build incremental delivery into your project then it raises the possibility of under-promising and over-delivering. Say you've identified that it would be possible to do three deliveries thus:

Delivery 1	July 31
Delivery 2	August 15
Delivery 3	August 31

Instead of telling your stakeholders this, promise them, for example:

Delivery 1	August 15
Delivery 2	August 31
Delivery 3	September 15

Now, if you can deliver to the original schedule, they'll love you. The Chilean mine rescue in 2010 was a stunning example of under-promise and over-deliver. In August when it was realised that the 33 miners were alive, it was said that it could take until Christmas to get them out. The miners were actually lifted to the surface over 12–13 October.

Example 3 Why contingency is mandatory

In Chapter 2, we talked about healthy and unhealthy projects and the three possible ways of dealing with changes. If you don't have contingency in your plan, because either:

● you didn't put it in in the first place; or

● you did, but then some genius took it out and you didn't stop them,

then you lose one of your three possible responses to changes. What this means in reality is that every change which occurs on your project which is *not* a big change will have to be dealt with by sucking it up, i.e. by working more hours. An unhealthy project? You betcha!

Example 4 Risk analysis for a company's business plan

Table 5.2 overleaf illustrates a risk analysis of a company's business plan. You will see from some of the risks (e.g. the first one) that the people who did it are being brutally honest. This obviously makes for the best kind of risk analysis!

This template also shows how easy it is to complete a risk analysis. Given the things it could potentially uncover, the 20 minutes or half-hour you spend doing a risk analysis could turn out to be one of the best investments of time you've ever made.

AND SO, WHAT SHOULD YOU DO?

1. Add contingency into all of your plans using the techniques we described in the 'How to' section.

2. Do risk analyses on all of your plans.

3. Maintain a 'top 10 risks' list and review it on a regular (weekly, monthly) basis.

Table 5.2 Risk analysis for a company's business plan

Risks	Likelihood	Impact	Exposure (Likelihood × Impact)	Actions	Indicators
1 Poor management by company's executives	2	3	6	• Performance review • Training • Quality assurance • Strengthen management team	• Departure from monthly plans/targets
2 Under-resourcing	3	3	9	• Verify targets against market data • Hire more people in January • Sort out existing staff's dance cards	• Departure from monthly plans/targets
3 Staff get sick	2	3	6	• Shadowing • Medicals for new employees • Sort out any existing problems	• Increase in monthly days lost due to sick leave
4 Lack of expertise	2	3	6	• Training and development • Proper and timely appraisals	• Things get screwed up
5 Office space blowout	1	1	1	• Begin looking for extra facilities	• People unable to find desks or conference/meeting facilities • Over-expenditure on external facilities
6 Revenues don't happen – forecast is wrong	2	3	6	• Weekly monitoring and change control • Financial and management reports	• Departure from monthly plans/targets
7 Competition	1	2	2	• Continue competitor watch	• New competitors identified

Risks	Likelihood	Impact	Exposure (Likelihood × Impact)	Actions	Indicators
8 Staff leave	1	3	3	• Ensure compensation and benefits packages are keeping pace with industry • Watch morale	• Staff exits look like exceeding acceptable attrition rate identified
9 Clients walk	1	3	3	• Renew CRM programme • Audits on lost customers	• Increase in complaints • Departure by established customers
10 Unrealistic goals	2	3	6	• Change control	• Departure from monthly plans/targets
11 Data security	3	3	9	• Discuss at special meeting	• Hacking • Breaches of firewalls • Theft
12 Brand fatigue	2	2	4	• Get Marketing to address and make a proposal	• Await Marketing's report
13 Cashflow	2	3	6	• Keep on it	• Departure from monthly plans/targets
14 Market changes	1	3	3	• Marketing to keep watching	• Departure from monthly plans/targets
15 Recession hits	1	3	3	• Run a tight ship – look for waste, unnecessary expenditure, etc.	• Departure from monthly plans/targets
16 New market distracts management	1	3	3	• Stick to plan	• Departure from monthly plans/targets

Chapter

Things either are or they aren't

How do you know if you're making progress towards your objective? Because things either are or they aren't; things are either done or not done. This chapter describes how to know when things are one or the other.

Questions

A couple of multiple choice questions this time:

1. Someone's working on a task for you. When asked how it's going they say they're '90 per cent done'. What does this mean?

   (a) He had 100 widgets to process, he's done 90 of them and so there are 10 left. Therefore he must be 90 per cent done.

   (b) He had 10 days to do the task and day 9 is about to come to an end. Therefore he must be 90 per cent done.

2. You are part of a project team. You finish a job several days early. Since this job is on the critical path (i.e. the shortest path through the project) this means that the project itself can be shortened by the same number of days. You go to the project manager and tell him. What is most likely to happen with this gift of several days that you hand him?

   (a) He'll give you something else to do to fill the several days.

   (b) Nothing. The several days will just get frittered away.

The rule

But before that, the answers to the questions. Question 1 – answer (a) is what the phrase '90 per cent done' *ought* to mean. Typically, in my experience, answer (b) is what it actually means. Question 2 – answer (a) almost certainly; answer (b) equally almost certainly, in my experience.

Okay – the rule. The rules we've talked about so far – rule 2, know what you're trying to do; 3, there is always a sequence of events; 4, things don't get done if people don't do them – provide a framework for getting things done. Our fifth rule, things rarely turn out as expected, points out that things will almost certainly turn out differently from the way rules 2 through 4 may have led us to believe. Given that this is so, we need a way of finding out how things are actually progressing.

As usual, the textbooks give us all sorts of ways – per cent complete, earned value, milestones passed, number of tasks complete, per cent of budget expended, the list is endless. But for us exponents of common sense, there is really only one measure that makes sense. That measure is to say that once we have our sequence of events, and once we know who's doing what, then each job on the sequence of events can exist only in one of two states. Either it's done or, failing that, it's not done. That is rule 6. Things either are or they aren't. Things are either done or they're not done. Jobs are either complete and therefore finished or they are not.

Now you may immediately object to this and say that you may be somewhere in the middle of something and that this is more useful information than to say 'it's not done'. However, to say that you're 'in the middle of something' is really not all that useful either. So can we do better than just saying 'I'm in the middle of something'?

"The trick is to break things down"

Once again, the trick is to break things down and, as we saw in Chapter 3, to do it in as much detail as possible.

If you're working on a two-month job, and you tell me that you're 'halfway through', then in almost all cases this really means nothing. However, if the two-month job can be thought of as being composed of, say, 10 or 15 smaller jobs, each of three or four days' duration, then you now actually tell me a lot of useful information.

If the first month is over and you tell me you're still working on job 1 out of 15, there's clearly a problem. Equally, if one month is over and you say to me that jobs 1 through 7 are done and you're now working on job 8, this tells an entirely different story. So too would telling me that after one month, only 1 job out of 15 remains to be done.

Since – it is hoped – you will have already built your sequence of events in as much detail as possible, it should be no great hardship to monitor progress in this way. If, of course, you don't put in this kind of detail, the job becomes something of a black box, where you have no clear idea what's going on inside. It's out of this lack of clarity that surprises and firefights are born. With black box jobs, you have no real early warning system.

Another issue here is the whole business of what constitutes 'done'. Here we can use rule 2, know what you're trying to do, to help us. In the same way that it is important to know for large projects or stratagems precisely what it is you're trying to achieve, it is also important to know this for each of the jobs in our sequence of events. Each job should produce some 'deliverable', something that we can look at or hold in our hand, and say 'yes, the existence of this thing means that this job is done'. So then the test of done or not done becomes a simple case of whether or not the deliverable exists.

How to

How are we doing?

The first of our tools is the one we have hinted at in the opening section. When assessing progress, we will think not in terms of part way through or 60 per cent done or any of these dodgy notions. Rather we will break a job down into elements (smaller jobs), and we will then record those jobs as being either done or not done. If somebody tries anything else, we will ask them to break the thing down into jobs which they then classify as either done or not done.

At first, people may find this notion a bit alien and you may have to coach them into understanding what you mean, what you want and why what you're asking for might actually make sense. I think you'll also find people motivated to break things down into smaller units of detail because of the following effect. Let's say you have weekly meetings whose purpose is to assess status. Somebody won't want to be coming week after week and reporting something as not done. Instead they will break it down into smaller components so that they can report progress from week to week.

Are things better or worse?

A variant on the notion of things either are or they aren't is the idea of whether things are better or worse. Things either are or they aren't is an instantaneous snapshot of the status of something. However, we may be interested in the *trend* – how the status of something is progressing over time. Let's say, for example, you run a company and it's experiencing cashflow difficulties. You are anxious to know some key indicators:

- Are costs decreasing?

- Are revenues increasing?

- What's happening to profits?

- How far am I in on my lines of credit?

Asking whether things are better or worse, from day to day, from week to week or from month to month, will help clarify for you what the trends are. Graphing the answer to the question 'Are things better or worse?' will make all of this abundantly clear.

Examples/Applications

Example 1 Monitoring progress

We have looked at the idea of breaking things down and then reporting the smaller jobs identified as being either done or not done. There is an additional aspect of this which is worth noting. Say, for example, you have a weekly status meeting where people must come and say how they're doing. (These comments apply equally well when the status is reported via progress reports rather than a meeting.) If someone is coming week after week and reporting that a particular job they're working on is not done, the pressure (peer or self-imposed) generated by this should cause them to focus more on getting the thing done, so that they can report that it's finished.

Example 2 Reducing stress #1

You can use this rule and rule 3, there is always a sequence of events, to help you reduce stress. We saw in Chapter 3 the idea of thinking of the sequence of events as a stack from which we took jobs as they needed to be done. One way we can consider each job is to say – using rule 6 – that either it must be done by us or it mustn't. Now, if we must do it, then let's go and do it. If not, somebody else must do it. In that case, there is nothing you can do about it, there's no point in worrying about it, so just wait until they get it done. (The Dalai Lama puts it succinctly like this: 'If a problem is fixable, if a situation is such that you can do something about it, then there is no need to worry. If it's not fixable, then there is no help in worrying. There is no benefit in worrying whatsoever.')

"Is there anything you can do to expedite the next job, even though it is theirs?"

A variation on this which makes it even more watertight is to do the following. When you've identified that the next move is theirs, ask yourself one additional question. Is there anything you can do to expedite the next job, even though it is theirs? If there is, this becomes a job in the stack for you. That being the case, you go and do it. If, however, there is genuinely nothing further you can do, then that's you off the hook until they get their bit done.

Example 3 Reducing stress #2

You can also reduce stress by checking whether things are better or worse than they were previously, thus establishing whether things have bottomed out. Are things going downhill or have they turned around and are starting to improve?

AND SO, WHAT SHOULD YOU DO?

Monitor progress on the basis of done or not done. Break things down to a lower level of detail where necessary.

Chapter

7

Look at things from others' points of view

In Chapter 1, we talked of seeing things simply. One simple way of seeing things is to see them from other people's points of view. Almost everything we undertake involves other people. Seeing things as they see them can be a powerful aid to understanding and getting things done.

Question

You've joined a new organisation and you've discovered that one of the people who works for you appears to be seriously overpaid for what he does. You know that he is pretty settled and happy in the organisation. You know also that he's fairly reasonable. You decide to reduce his salary to that of his peers. Your analysis is that while he might be very upset about it initially, he will eventually see your point of view and the whole thing will blow over. Is this what actually happens?

(a) Yes, it's all about how settled and happy he is in the organisation. That plus the fact that he's a reasonable person.

(b) He goes ballistic. He quits and you end up with a lawsuit on your hands.

(c) It's stormier than you had expected. You have to give a bit and not implement as big a reduction as you had been planning. Then it passes.

(d) You sleep on it, wake up the next day and decide this was a crazy idea. You've got plenty on your plate without drawing this on yourself. You let sleeping dogs lie.

The rule

First, the question. If you think that anything other than answer (b) is the right answer, you need to spend more time empathising with people.

The final rule is a very old one. Interestingly, it is also common to a number of the world's major religions.

For example, you may know of the Talmud, the 20-volume work that can be thought of as an 'encyclopaedia' of Judaism. The Talmud tells the story of a Gentile who comes to a Rabbi and asks to be taught all of Judaism while standing on one foot. One of the Rabbi's students has the man driven from the Rabbi's door, taking the question to be impertinent or mocking. Unperturbed, the Rabbi replies: 'What is offensive to you do not do to others. That is the core of Judaism. The rest is commentary. Now carry on your studies.'

Buddhism also has a view on this rule. Here is the Dalai Lama on the subject: 'I think that empathy is important not only as a means of enhancing compassion, but I think that generally speaking, when dealing with others on any level, if you're having some difficulties, it's extremely helpful to be able to try to put yourself in the other person's place and see how you would react to the situation.'

Finally, the notion of 'do as you would be done to' is one that is widely known in the Christian faith.

"If people are positive and well motivated, they will move mountains"

The six rules we have looked at so far are very much about getting things done. More than anything else, the thing that will determine how easy or difficult things are to get done will be how people react to them. If people are positive and well motivated, they will move mountains. On the other hand, if people are not well disposed towards what is being attempted, they will, in an extreme case, bring it to a halt.

The rule, then, is simple. See things from other people's viewpoints and modify your plans and/or behaviour, if necessary, to maximise your chances of success. Precisely how you do this is the subject of the next section.

How to

Put yourself in their shoes

Once again, we can quote the Dalai Lama who describes this technique very simply and elegantly. He says: 'This technique involves the capacity to temporarily suspend insisting on your own viewpoint but rather to look from the other person's perspective, to imagine what would be the situation if you were in his shoes, how you would deal with this. This helps you develop an awareness and respect for another's feelings, which is an important factor in reducing conflicts and problems with other people.'

My editor, Rachael Stock, has put it another way, but no less eloquently: 'Never assume you know everything.' Or to put it another way still: 'Be open to learning from others.' Finally, the point is also made by Stephen Covey in his bestselling *The 7 Habits of Highly Effective People*. One of Covey's '7 habits' is to 'think win/win'.

Maximise the win-conditions of the stakeholders

We saw this concept in Chapter 2, when we looked at the 'know if what you're trying to do is what everyone wants' tool. Just to remind you, the stakeholders are all those people affected by what you're intending to do. Each of those stakeholders will have a set of win-conditions. Win-conditions are those things that they want to get from the particular venture or undertaking. It is quite likely that the various win-conditions will not be compatible with one another. Anyone who has even a nodding acquaintance with the peace talks in Northern Ireland or in the Middle East should have no problem understanding this concept. So, given that the various win-conditions are often more or less incompatible, this tool is about trying to find a set of win-conditions that everyone can live with. You'll remember we described a way of doing this in Chapter 2, Example 1.

Examples/Applications

Example 1 Meetings revisited

Using all of our rules, we can now see how to conduct a decent meeting. We can also use our rules to spot when we've been landed with a turkey – a meeting that will consume everybody's time and be of little value, if any.

To conduct a meeting, you need to do the following:

1. Figure out the objective(s) of the meeting (rule 2, know what you're trying to do).

2. Identify the bunch of things that have to get done to get you to the objective(s) (rule 3, there is always a sequence of events).

3. Identify who should attend. People are going to have to do those things (rule 4, things don't get done if people don't do them). Thus rules 3 and 4 identify who's got to come to the meeting.

4. Build the agenda. Rules 3 and 4 also enable us to build the agenda, including a time constraint on each

item. Using rule 5, things rarely turn out as expected, add in some contingency to give the time constraint on the meeting as a whole.

5. Publish the objective(s), agenda and time constraints, and indicate to each participant what preparation, if any, is required from them (rule 7, look at things from others' points of view).

6. Hold the meeting, driving it to the agenda and time constraints you have identified (rule 4, things don't get done if people don't do them).

7. Prepare an action list arising from the meeting (rule 3, there is always a sequence of events).

8. Stop when the time is up. By then, if you've done your job properly, the objective(s) should have been met.

To spot a turkey, do the following. When you are asked to come to a meeting, ask:

● What is the objective?

● Why do you need to go? In other words, what leads them to believe that you can contribute anything useful?

● What preparation do you have to do?

● How long will it last?

If you can't get sensible answers to all of these questions, you're probably on to a loser. Assuming you're a person who espouses the virtues of common sense then you should simply not go. If you wanted to pass on that common sense to the other people, you could write an email explaining why.

Example 2 Status reporting

In status reporting there seem to be two schools of thought: tell 'em nothing and tell 'em everything. Interestingly, the two schools have something in common – both types of report can result in you not getting any information at all on the status of things. In the first case, this is because they didn't actually give you any, while in the second, it's because they overwhelmed you with so much stuff that it's impossible to see the wood for the trees. Rule 7 tells us that we *have* to tell others what we're doing. It doesn't say we must tell everybody 100 per cent of everything, but it does say that we can't tell them nothing.

"We must filter what we're saying in some way"

Now if we're not going to tell 100 per cent, what are we going to do? Well, we must filter what we're saying in some way, but not so much that the message is garbled, misunderstood, hidden, reversed or lied about. In my experience, the majority of traditional status reports, whether written or verbal, do all of these things. In general, such status reports give the impression that there are impressive amounts of stuff happening – we did this, we did that, this happened, that happened. (The message is: 'We're earning our money.') Not everything that happens is good stuff, so status reports are always keen to report bad incidents that have occurred. (The message is: 'We're *really* earning our money.') But there's always the almost compulsory happy ending, the feeling that in spite of everything, we're going to be OK. In other words, few status reports are prepared to report bad news.

In general, people are interested in one or more of the following aspects of what you're doing:

- Will I get everything I thought I was going to get and, if not, what can I expect?

- Is it on time and, if not, what can I now expect?

- How's it doing as regards costs – Over? Under? About right?

- Will the thing I get meet my needs?

In reporting the status, you need to tell them about the things they are interested in. And you need to tell them both the instantaneous status – here's how it is today – and what the status is over time – in other words, the trend. Only then can they have a true picture of how things are going. By truthfully reporting the trend, they can understand not just the kind of shape we're in today but also how things might unfold in the future. The result will be no surprises in store for anybody.

Finally, who are we talking about here? Well, all of the stakeholders, as we've defined them earlier. In general, there are at least four that we can always regard as being present. The first is you, the person responsible for getting the thing done; next is your team, the people who are doing the work; third is the customer, for whom the work is being done; and finally, your boss. All of these need to be given an insight – though not necessarily the same one – into how things are proceeding.

First, you need to understand that status yourself. Rule 6, things either are or they aren't, will help you here. Once you know, by considering the status from other people's points of view (rule 7, look at things from others' points of view), you will be able to deliver the status to them. It will be a message that they can understand (because it is expressed in terms that are real to them), that gives the status (because it tells the truth) and that will seek to clarify rather than obscure how things are going.

Table 7.1 opposite gives an example of some extracts from a status report. The extracts illustrate both instantaneous status and one possible trend we might be interested in.

Example 3 Some stress management techniques

Keep a sense of proportion (or, there is always someone worse off than you)

This one comes to us courtesy of the 'are things better or worse?' tool in Chapter 6. In general, no matter how bleak your situation may be, it is almost certainly true that there is someone in the world worse off than you. Every day, thousands of people die of hunger, disease, torture, execution, neglect, abuse, loneliness. Most of the things we face don't add up to a hill of beans in the context of these problems. The next time you're feeling stressed, pick up the paper or turn on the television news.

"It is almost certainly true that there is someone in the world worse off than you"

See it a year from now

Rule 7 tells us to look at things from others' points of view. Imagine yourself a year from now. How will the issue that is causing you so much worry seem a year from now? Will you actually be able to remember it? Visualise it and see if this brings anything new.

Table 7.1 Status report

STATUS REPORT

Project:	Great Product Version 1.2
Report:	14
Date:	21 October 2011
Project Manager:	Frank
Team:	Rachel, Debbie, Declan, Steve, Mary
Distribution:	As above plus
	Bernadette, Hugh, Dan, Pedro, Ted
	File + tell anyone else who's interested

Overall status:

Requirements	Design	Development	Testing	Limited customer release
Complete	Complete	Complete	In progress	Not yet started

Current dates are:

Testing to complete on 17 November 2011

General availability (at end of limited customer release) –
19 January 2012

TRENDS

Delivery date – change history

Date of change	Reason for change	Into beta date	General availability date
	Original dates	1 May 2011	1 Sep 2011
9 May 2011	See section 1 of the project plan	24 Nov 2011	23 Jan 2012
27 May 2011	Added an extra person for a couple of weeks	14 Nov 2011	12 Jan 2012
1 July 2011	Some improvements due to use of Mary	3 Nov 2011	5 Jan 2012
14 Oct 2011	Slip in development schedule	17 Nov 2011	19 Jan 2012

The marathon runner

I used to run marathons (not very well, I should add). Now I think you'll agree that the notion of running 26 and a bit miles is ridiculous. It's outrageous. And so, rather than thinking about all the appalling stuff that lies up ahead, marathon runners use – whether they know it or not – rule 3, there is always a sequence of events. Don't worry about the stuff that lies way off in the future. Rather, work your way through the next little job in the sequence. In the case of marathon runners, this means making the next telegraph pole, or tree, or mile marker or feeding station. Then turn your attention to the next stage of the journey.

Talk to somebody

Rule 7 again. Also, as the old saying goes, 'A problem shared is a problem halved.'

Example 4 Assessing things – projects and project plans

"Common sense can help us chart a way through the mass of data"

Increasingly, one of the things you may be required to do is to assess plans that are being proposed or undertakings that are actually in progress. For example, a subcontractor may be presenting a plan for something that has been outsourced to them. Or you may be asked to make a recommendation on a business plan or the proposed funding of a particular venture. Or the venture may already be in progress and the question is how well or otherwise it is doing. Often these days, these things we are being asked to make a decision on are highly technical or complex, and we may not be personally familiar with the technicalities or complexities. How, then, do we make the right decision? Our rules of common sense can help us chart a way through the mass of data and unearth the nuggets of information we really need.

It seems to me that sometimes people refer to this as 'gut feel' or 'gut instinct'. Gut feel is not a wild stab in the dark but a sense or a feeling that the odds are in your favour. The following is a way of trying to assess those odds.

Imagine you are at a presentation about, or reading a report on, or considering some venture that is occurring on the ground. What do you need to look for?

1. Rule 2, know what you're trying to do, tells us that somewhere in the welter of information there had better be some sort of goal or objective to this thing. This goal must have two main characteristics. First, it must be well defined, i.e. it should be possible to tell, quite unambiguously, when this goal will have been achieved. There should be no confusion or fuzziness about whether or not we will have crossed the finish line. For example, confusion among the stakeholders as to what constituted the end would be a classic breach of this requirement. The other thing is that the goal must be current, i.e. any changes to it that have occurred along the way should have been accumulated and now be part of the final goal.

2. Rule 3, there is always a sequence of events, says that somewhere we should be able to see the series of activities that bring us through the project from where we are now to the goal. This sequence of events could be represented in many forms, and we have seen some of them in this book:

- a Gantt chart – who-does-what-when;

- a spreadsheet – who-spends/earns-what-when.

3. The level of detail of the sequence of events must be such as to convince us that somebody has analysed, in so far as they can, all the things that need to be done in this project. Pretty, computer-generated, high-level charts don't cut the mustard – unless they can show you the supporting detail.

4. Rule 4, things don't get done if people don't do them, says that there had better be someone leading the venture, and all of the jobs in the sequence of events better have people's names against them. Also, people's availability must be clear. Names aren't enough. We need to know how much of those people's time is available to work on this venture. Notice that with points (2) and (3) it should be possible to do a quick calculation that will test the venture to its core. Point (2) should tell you how much work has to be done, (3) should tell you how much work is available, i.e. how many people for how much of their time. These two numbers should essentially be the same.

5. Rule 5, things rarely turn out as expected. If the venture has no contingency or margin for error in it, send them home with a flea in their ear!

Example 5 Build a fast-growing company

In the 6 September 1999 edition of *Fortune*, there was an article on America's fastest growing companies. The article identified seven factors that these companies had in common. Perhaps, at this stage, it should come as no surprise to us that behind these seven factors we can clearly see our rules.

These were the factors:

1. The companies always deliver on their commitments (rule 7, look at things from others' points of view). If somebody is a customer of yours then, despite the way it may seem at times, they don't actually expect miracles. (No, really, it's true!) What they do expect, and rightly so, is that you will deliver on whatever they have been led to believe and meet whatever expectations have been set for them.

2. They don't overpromise (rule 7, look at things from others' points of view – again). This is really not too different from the preceding one. In the article, this factor was related specifically to what companies were promising to deliver – and subsequently did deliver – to the financial community/Wall Street.

3. They sweat the small stuff (rule 3, there is always a sequence of events). If you remember, a lot of what we talked about in Chapter 3 was about trying to understand the detail of what needed to happen. These days, in a lot of cases, time is an even more valuable commodity than money. Knowing where our time goes, ensuring that it is spent wisely, removing time wasters, and avoiding having to firefight things which should never have been firefights in the first place, is what this one is all about.

4. They build a fortress. This one is about protecting your business, especially by creating barriers to entry (rule 5, things rarely turn out as expected). Just because things are going well doesn't mean they'll always go well. Maintaining a healthy insecurity about things, always having some contingency in the bag and keeping a watchful eye on the top 10 risks will

ensure that your fortress becomes as impregnable as possible to attack.

5. They create a culture (rule 2, know what you're trying to do). This factor is about the corporate cultures that these fast-growth companies have created. In all of the cases cited, the companies set out deliberately to create a certain kind of culture, be it a very formal one, as in the case of Siebel Systems, or an informal one like casual-clothes maker, American Eagle.

6. They learn from their mistakes (rule 3, there is always a sequence of events/record of what actually happens).

7. They shape their story. This again is about ensuring that the investors/financial analysts never feel uncertain about a company, but rather are kept in the loop by the company as to what is going on. Again it's about rule 7, look at things from others' points of view. As the article says: 'When there is uncertainty with this kind of small, growing company, the first thing people do is run … And when one money manager sees someone else bailing out, his first thought is: "What does that guy know that I don't?" They don't wait around to find out what's really going on.'

Example 6 Presentations

"Make sure it's worth listening to"

You know how busy you are. Everyone else is that busy too – never enough time and so many things to be done. Now, if people are going to give up some of their incredibly scarce time to come and listen to something you say, then you damn well better make sure it's worth listening to.

I don't know how you've found it, but in my experience good presentations are something of a rarity. Instead I've seen plenty of presenters and presentations that were any of: smug, patronising, aggressive, incomprehensible, unconvincing, rambling, scared, verbose, ran on too long, bored the audience silly, too casual, dishonest, or unsure of their material. The presenter who is authoritative, interesting, relaxed, maybe humorous or dramatic, who believes in what they say, and who communicates that belief, is still something of an oasis in the desert when you come across them.

While you'll always learn something useful at them, you don't have to have attended umpteen presentation skills courses to be a good presenter. Common sense shows you what you have to do to make a good presentation.

1. Rule 7, look at things from others' points of view, starts us in the right place. People are going to give up their time to come to this presentation. Why is that going to be a useful thing for them to do? Presumably they're going to learn something that is to their advantage. But, you may say, I'm making a sales presentation, I'm trying to sell them, something, not educate them. Uh-uh, I don't think so. I make sales presentations all the time. And the best ones are those where I set out to teach my audience something and then, somewhere in the midst of it all, put in the sales messages. How many pure sales presentations have you been to that you remember? Okay, so this is the first point: you're going to tell them something that is to their advantage. If at all possible, ask members of the audience some time in advance of the presentation what they are hoping to get from it. This obviously

maximises the chances that you will actually give them that. You can do this right up to the moment you're about to begin; however, the earlier you do it the more time you have to prepare.

2. Rule 2, know what you're trying to do. Okay, you've decided you're going to tell them something to their advantage. Now you need to decide precisely what your main messages are. And since it is also well known that people can't remember too many things, you'd better make sure that you have only a handful of main messages.

3. Rule 3, there is always a sequence of events. Now decide the sequence in which you are going to tell them the messages. Research has shown that the human brain primarily remembers the following:

- items from the beginning of the learning period ('the primacy effect');

- items from the end of the learning period ('the recency effect');

- items which are emphasised as being in some way outstanding or unique.

Of course you didn't need research to tell you this. It's known through the great adage for all presenters:

- tell 'em what you're gonna tell 'em;

- tell 'em;

- tell 'em what you told 'em.

Again, research has shown that people remember those items which are of particular interest to them, hence the value of understanding in advance what it is they want to know. This also tells us that we should try to present each of our points from a point of view that our listeners can relate to (rule 7, look at things from others' points of view).

4. Rule 5, things rarely turn out as expected. So anticipate the questions that might get asked. If you can't, have a dry run – this will throw them up anyway. Questions can often take you down paths you hadn't intended to go, and deliver messages you didn't intend to deliver. A dry run will help you spot these trapdoors and close them. Questions also highlight points where your presentation is weak or prone to misunderstanding or is unclear, and so are invaluable in terms of improving the presentation next time you give it. That is, of course, if you view questions in this way – as a learning opportunity. Not everyone does!

5. Now do it. Use the adage of 'First things first' to deliver your key messages at the beginning. Work your way through the rest of it. Then remind them of the key messages at the end.

AND SO, WHAT SHOULD YOU DO?

1. When you are undertaking anything, remember that in almost all cases, other people will be affected by what you do. See if you can ensure that you identify who those people are, what their views and needs are, and how much you can take these into account.

2. If at all possible, when planning something, try to involve the people who will do the work.

Afterword

Remembering the rules of common sense – one way

I've tried, in the course of the book, to keep reminding you of the seven rules of common sense:

1	Many things are simple
2	Know what you're trying to do
3	There is always a sequence of events
4	Things don't get done if people don't do them
5	Things rarely turn out as expected
6	Things either are or they aren't
7	Look at things from others' points of view

Here is perhaps another way to think of them:

- The first and last can be thought of as over-arching rules. Keep things simple and see them from other viewpoints.

- Rule 2 is about knowing what you're trying to achieve.

- Rules 3 through 6 are built around the sequence of events which is how we accomplish what it is we're trying to achieve.

Remembering the rules of common sense – another way

(a) In general, rather than looking for complicated ways to do things, we're going to do the opposite. Rule 1, many things are simple.

(b) In considering any venture/undertaking/project, we need to understand what it is we're trying to do. Rule 2, know what you're trying to do.

(c) Once we know what we're trying to do, rule 3, there is always a sequence of events involved in doing it.

(d) The sequence of events happens only if people do the jobs in the sequence. Rule 4, things don't get done if people don't do them.

(e) No matter how well thought out the sequence of events is, there are always surprises. Rule 5, things rarely turn out as expected.

(f) As our sequence of events unfolds, jobs in the sequence are either complete or they are not. Rule 6, things either are or they aren't.

(g) As well as keeping things simple, we should always, rule 7, look at things from others' points of view.

Practising common sense – one way

It'll all be a bit pointless – me writing it, you reading it, I mean – if you don't do something as a result. Conveniently – because it wasn't deliberate on my part – we have ended up with seven rules of common sense. Thus one way you could begin to remember them and, more importantly, to apply them would be to concentrate on a different one every day of the week.

- *Mondays* (rule 1, many things are simple). Focus on trying to keep things simple. Try to plan for an uncomplicated day with not as much rushing around as normal. At meetings, if things look like they're getting too complicated, drag the participants back to a simpler view of things. Ask yourself constantly, 'Is this as simple as it could be?' Perhaps extend the simplicity to other areas of your life – what you wear, what you eat, how you get to work, how much garbage you generate, how much of the world's resources you use. Take a 'simple pleasure' that you enjoy and make space for it in the day. Take something that you normally do that day and try to find a simpler way of doing it. Try something off the 'And so, what should you do?' list on page 10. Take something that you think/suspect doesn't add much value to your job (e.g. a meeting or report) and don't do it today. See if the sky falls in. If it does, then the thing really did add value. But if the sky didn't fall and nobody much noticed, then maybe you won't have to do this thing again. Or ever! Nice!

- *Tuesdays* (rule 2, know what you're trying to do). Have an objective that you're trying to achieve today and achieve it no matter what. Any meetings you go to, calls you make, presentations you give, understand in advance what you're hoping to get from them. Review at the end of the day how you did. Try something off the 'And so, what should you do?' list on page 25.

- *Wednesdays* (rule 3, there is always a sequence of events). Think in terms of sequences of events. Align the things you intend to do today with the bigger goals you have identified for yourself. To put it another way, are the jobs you intend to do today taken from the stacks of your various undertakings?

After meetings, calls or conversations, ensure that things aren't left hanging there, but that everybody is clear what is going to happen next. Try something off the 'And so, what should you do?' list on page 52.

- *Thursdays* (rule 4, things don't get done if people don't do them). From a personal point of view, focus on getting the things you intended to get done, done. Review how you fared at the end of the day. How did things actually pan out? Did you achieve what you set out to achieve or did other things intervene? If the latter, what can you learn from today and what can you do to ensure that this doesn't happen to you again? If you have people doing things for you, are they clear what needs to be done? Are you happy that they've thought through their sequences of events and have ample time to do what they've promised? Use dance cards on them if they're having problems, because their problems will eventually become *your* problems. Try something off the 'And so, what should you do?' list on page 76.

- *Fridays* (rule 5, things rarely turn out as expected). Ask yourself whether there are contingencies in place on all of your key projects. Have you done a risk analysis on them? If not, do one. If you have, review the top 10 risks and see if you're doing all you can to mitigate them. Try something off the 'And so, what should you do?' list on page 89.

- *Saturdays* (or, if you only want to be a common-sense person five days a week, then wait until Monday and pick it up from there; rule 6, things either are or they aren't). If you're at home, then this will probably raise (uncomfortable?) questions about the status of that do-it-yourself job that's been outstanding for a long time;

the washing or the cooking for next week; the home-work assignment for the course you're doing; or things to do with the children. If you've chosen the five-day week common sense, then keep the focus on whether or not things are really done, and if people are claiming they are, how they can prove it. Try the advice in the 'And so, what should you do?' section on page 101.

- *Sundays* (rule 7, look at things from others' points of view). Not a bad thing to do any day of the week. Spend a little time seeing the world as somebody else sees it – your partner, child, parent, employer, boss, subordinate, team member, peer, work colleague, family member, friend. You may be surprised what you'll learn. Try something off the 'And so, what should you do? list on page 121.

Practising common sense – another way

Rule 2, know what you're trying to do, and rule 3, there is always a sequence of events, provide very powerful ways of tackling any problem. It goes like this. Establish what it is you're trying to do, using rule 2. Now ask yourself, using rule 3, what the starting point is. What is the first job in the sequence of events? Now, again using rule 3, ask yourself what happens next. What's the next job in the sequence of events, the next link in the chain? As you iden-tify each job, some of our rules may offer further insights.

Carry on like this until you have established an unbroken sequence of jobs from where you are now to where you want to be.

And finally, good luck!

Bibliography

This list includes all the references within individual chapters, as well as a few other publications I consulted during the writing of this book.

Boehm, Barry W. & Ross, Rony (1989) 'Theory-W software project management: rules and examples', *IEEE Transactions on Software Engineering*, Vol. 15, No. 7, July, 902–16

Buzan, Tony (2009) *The Mind Map Book: Unlock Your Creativity, Boost Your Memory, Change Your Life*, London: BBC Active

Carroll, Lewis (2003) *Alice's Adventures in Wonderland And Through the Looking-Glass*, London: Penguin Classics

Charan, Ram & Colvin, Geoffrey (2001) 'Managing for the slowdown', *Fortune*, 5 February

Chopra, Deepak (1996) *The Seven Spiritual Laws of Success*, London: Transworld Publishers

Cooper, Alan (1999) *The Inmates are Running the Asylum*, Indianapolis, IN: Sams

Covey, Stephen R. (1989) *The 7 Habits of Highly Effective People*, London: Simon & Schuster

De Bono, Edward (1971) *Lateral Thinking for Management*, Harmondsworth: Penguin Books

De Bono, Edward (1999) *Simplicity*, Harmondsworth: Penguin Books

DeMarco, Tom (1997) *The Deadline*, New York: Dorset House Publishing

Dickens, Charles (2003) *Oliver Twist*, London: Penguin Books

Eberts, Jake & Ilott, Terry (1990) *My Indecision is Final*, London: Faber and Faber

European Commission, Opinion of the Consumer Committee adopted on 8 December, 1998 on the reform of the Common Agricultural Policy

Fisher, Roger & Ury, William (1981) *Getting to Yes*, London: Hutchinson Business

Gelb, Michael (1998) *How to Think Like Leonardo Da Vinci*, London: Thorsons

Gilb, Tom (1988) *Principles of Software Engineering Management*, London: Addison-Wesley

Gladwell, Malcolm (2000) *The Tipping Point: How Little Things Can Make a Big Difference*, London: Little Brown

Hamel, Gary (2000) 'Reinvent your company', *Fortune*, 12 June

Hampton, Henry & Freyer, Steve (1992) *Voices of Freedom*, New York: Bantam

His Holiness The Dalai Lama (1999) *Ancient Wisdom, Modern World*, London: Little Brown

His Holiness The Dalai Lama & Cutler, Howard C. (1998) *The Art of Happiness*, New York: Riverhead Books

Hoff, Benjamin (1994) *The Tao of Pooh and the Te of Piglet*, London: Methuen

Kellaway, Lucy (2000) *Sense and Nonsense in the Office*, London: Financial Times Prentice Hall

Lovell, Jim & Kluger, Jeffrey (1994) *Apollo 13*, New York: Pocket Books

Nalty, Bernard C. & Prichard, Russell A. (1999) *D-Day: 'Operation Overlord' from its Planning to the Liberation of Paris*, Conshohocken, PA: Combined Books

Nicholl, Charles (2004) *Leonardo Da Vinc: The Flights of the Mind*, London: Penguin

O'Connell, Fergus (2000) *How to Run Successful Projects in Web Time*, Boston, MA: Artech House

O'Connell, Fergus (2001) *How to Run Successful Projects: The Silver Bullet*, Addison-Wesley

Schrage, Michael (2000) 'The broadband promise: every e-mail a Spielberg epic', *Fortune*, Fall, Special Issue

Schumacher, Ernst F. (1989) *Small is Beautiful: Economics as if People Mattered*, London: HarperCollins

Schwartz, Nelson D. (1999) 'Secrets of Fortune's fastest-growing companies', *Fortune*, 6 September

Shapiro, Eileen (1998) *The Seven Deadly Sins of Business*, Oxford: Capstone

Smith, Preston G. & Reinersten, Donald G. (1998) *Developing Products in Half the Time*, New York: Wiley

Winkler, John (1989) *Winning Sales and Marketing Tactics*, Oxford: Butterworth Heinemann

Wouk, Herman (1988) *This is My God*, London: Little Brown

Index